Extraordinary Power for Ordinary Christians

Transforming Mere Man Into Instruments of God's Glory

Erik Tammaru

Treasure House

An Imprint of

Destiny Image® Publishers, Inc.
P.O. Box 310
Shippensburg, PA 17257-0310

"For where your treasure is,
there will your heart be also." Matthew 6:21

ISBN 1-56043-309-4

For Worldwide Distribution.
Printed in the U.S.A.

This book and all other Destiny Image, Revival Press,
and Treasure House books are available
at Christian bookstores and distributors worldwide.

For a U.S. bookstore nearest you, call **1-800-722-6774**.
For more information on foreign distributors, call **717-532-3040**.
Or reach us on the Internet: **http://www.reapernet.com**

Acknowledgments

Someone once said that we are who we are because of the grace of God and because of what others have invested in us. I recognize that if it weren't for God's grace and mercy in my life and for the many wonderful men and women of God that He's brought into my life, there would be no book. Most of what is contained in this book is a direct result of their leadership, mentoring, and friendship.

To Don Glab—Thanks for reaching out to a newborn Christian.

To Jim and Patti Wilson—Thanks for believing in me and helping us to succeed in marriage and in life.

To Chip Ward—Thanks for being a great pastor and for releasing us into leadership.

To Grant and Karin Layman—Thanks for letting us go for it with the college group and E-Team!

To Ché Ahn—Thanks for your discipleship and example of a man consumed with a passion to preach the gospel.

To Ken and Debbie Roberts and to Jim and Marcia Walter—Thanks for modeling what it means to lead a large church with a genuine pastor's heart and for believing in us and our mission from the beginning.

To Larry Tomczak—Thanks for being a father and hero to us in faith and for lighting the fire in us to reach the nations.

To Jon Palmer—Thanks for your friendship and your passion to build churches in Europe and for taking a chance on us "Americans" in Vienna.

To the members of Oikos International Church—Thanks for gladly receiving us with such love.

To Mom and Dad Tammaru—Thanks for always praying for me, even during the difficult times, for modeling a good marriage, and for your active help in our mission.

Most of all, to my wife Crissy and the kids, who are living the adventure with me—Thank you for your love, support, and willingness to go wherever God will send us, even at great personal sacrifice. This book is dedicated to you.

Endorsements

"We are living in a time when God is challenging many men and women to new levels of faith and courage. *Extraordinary Power for Ordinary Christians* will inspire you to rise to a new level and enjoy the adventure along the way."

Ken L. Roberts, Senior Pastor
North Coast Church, Cleveland, Ohio

"*Extraordinary Power for Ordinary Christians* is a Holy Spirit manual to a life of excitement and exploits for God. If you mean business about finding and fulfilling your destiny as a Christian, this book is a must! Having known Erik Tammaru for over a decade, I highly recommend this book and the man who wrote it. Let's all move in 'extraordinary power'!"

Larry Tomczak
Pastor, Author, and Speaker

"Erik's book was delightful to read. His many experiences, from being a policeman to becoming a pastor, will inspire and encourage any believer who longs to follow Jesus into his or her destiny! This book will help you become a fisher of men in the great harvest now coming to the earth."

Rick Wright, Pastor
Harvest International Ministries

Contents

Foreword

There has never been a more exciting time to be alive. The manifest presence of God is being released around the globe. His unmistakable power is being poured over the earth, and miracles, signs, and wonders are bursting forth as revival swells are growing.

God has apportioned to every one of us a part of this blessing—and it is the greatest fulfillment of purpose and joy that we could ever conceive. It is ours for the taking—provided we grasp and do what He has planned with the tools and direction that He has already provided. Quite simply, we are called to live a faith that rattles chains and shakes the earth and share a gospel that sets the hearts of people free. Erik Tammaru has a practical grasp of how to embrace and live in this reality. This book is his gift to you.

I have had the privilege of mentoring Erik through the early years of his spiritual walk, as well as walking alongside him as God has sent him to the nations. He is a man of integrity who understands the power of the Holy Spirit and intimacy with God that produces changed lives, and he knows how to share it.

Take hold of this new day for evangelism and the fulfillment of your faith. Expect a life of the supernatural, and it shall be yours. Rise up and live the adventure to which you were called! You will never regret it!

Dr. Ché H. Ahn, Senior Pastor
Harvest Rock Church, Pasadena, California

Preface

I consider myself to be a pretty ordinary guy. Like 98 percent of all Christians, I'm not famous or renowned. I have a job, a wife, five children, and I experience everyday struggles and joys just like you. Most of us have read accounts of remarkable people—extremely gifted people—who have seen extraordinary power at work in their lives and ministries. We've heard about Finney, Wigglesworth, Whitefield, Roberts, and others from the past. Today, names like Wimber, Howard-Browne, Arnott, and Hinn are widely known. But what about you and me? Can we dare to believe God in our ordinary existences for similar power and results? My answer to this question is a resounding, "Yes!" If you consider yourself "ordinary," or "average," this book is written with you in mind.

Yes, it's true that I'm a pastor now, but most of the stories and examples that I've included in this book are from the times in my life when I worked a "regular" job. Actually, it's been my experience that God often works more powerfully *outside* of the four walls of a church than He does on the inside. It's my prayer that as you read this book, you will be challenged and inspired to climb out of the mundane and into the supernatural realm! You *can* be used by God today to impact your world! You *can* see your family and friends come to Christ! You *can* live the exciting adventure of a Spirit-led life! I believe we are in the days when God is raising up an army of supernatural Christians composed of ordinary people. He wants to take people like us and use us to do mighty exploits! The apostle Paul once wrote:

*Brothers, think of what you were when you were called. Not many of you were **wise** by human standards; not many were **influential**; not many were of **noble** birth. But God chose the **foolish** things of the world to shame the wise; God chose the **weak** things of the world to shame the **strong*** (1 Corinthians 1:26-27).

According to that definition, we all qualify for service in God's end-time army. Are you ready to get started on a new adventure? ***Today*** can mark a new beginning in your *ordinary* life!

Part One

Transforming Our Hearts

Let us draw near to God with a sincere heart in full assurance of faith, having our hearts sprinkled to cleanse us from a guilty conscience and having our bodies washed with pure water (Hebrews 10:22).

Test me, O Lord, and try me, examine my heart and my mind; for Your love is ever before me, and I walk continually in Your truth (Psalm 26:2-3).

Chapter One

Divine Imperative

The tires of police cruiser number 889 squealed on the hot pavement as I turned into the townhouse parking lot. It was a typically muggy summer evening in the Washington, D.C., suburbs, the kind of weather that normally brought out the worst in people and kept a police officer hopping. This evening was unusually slow, however, and I had taken advantage of the temporary lull to visit a friend from church. I stood on Paul's doorstep in the stifling humidity, but received no response to my knocks. Just as I was returning to my cruiser, Paul came running up from a nearby field.

"Hey Erik, wait!" he yelled, a little out of breath from running. "I was just playing baseball with some neighborhood kids. Want to come in for a drink?"

A few minutes later, as Paul and I were seated at his kitchen table enjoying tall glasses of iced tea, there was a knock at the front door.

"I wonder who that could be?" Paul said, as he got up to answer it. Opening the door, he was greeted by a handsome young man with a winning smile.

"Good evening, sir," the man grinned, reaching out to shake Paul's hand. "My name is Leroy, and I would really like the opportunity to share a special offer with you." Paul, always the nice guy, invited him in.

As they walked into the kitchen, my walkie-talkie sitting on the table was screeching out different police codes. Drawn by the sound, Leroy took one look at me and snapped to attention as if he were addressing a drill sergeant.

"Good evening, sir!" I almost expected him to salute. Instead, he took my hand in a crushing grip and said, "Allow me to introduce myself, sir. My name is Leroy, and I would like the opportunity…"

At that moment, the Lord spoke to my heart. *Share your testimony with him.* Immediately, a struggle began within me. *Not now! Lord, this is my break. It's really hot. I just want to drink my tea in peace and fellowship with Paul. Besides, this guy's probably not even interested! What would he think about some crazy cop telling him about Jesus?*

Again the Holy Spirit nudged me. *Share your testimony with him.* Leroy was halfway into his sales pitch when he told us of his personal goal of becoming a millionaire by the time he was 30. I leapt at the opening.

"Leroy," I smiled, trying not to look too intimidating in my uniform. "It's admirable that you have such ambition and goals for your life, but have you ever thought about eternal security? For example, what would happen to you if you died tonight? Where would you go?"

Leroy's confident look evaporated. "Uh…," he stammered. "I hope I would go to Heaven, but I'm not really sure…."

As the simmering heat of the evening melted the ice in our tea, so the heat of God's conviction melted Leroy's cool facade. Drops of perspiration appeared on his brow as he acknowledged his uncertainty of things eternal. He forgot all about his sales pitch. For ten minutes, Paul and I shared our faith with Leroy, and then he knelt down on Paul's kitchen floor and prayed to receive Christ as his Lord and Savior! There was no doubt that this was from the Lord! Clearly God had orchestrated circumstances to bring me, Paul, and Leroy together at that place and time for the express purpose of ushering Leroy into His Kingdom!

Police business drew me abruptly back to the beat, leaving Paul to finish up with Leroy. The sun was setting when I got back into my cruiser and turned onto U.S. Highway 29. What had begun as a routine and uneventful night on the job, God had transformed into an awesome and exciting demonstration of His grace and glory!

* * *

A few days later, Paul mailed Leroy a letter encouraging him in his new faith and included his phone number and a list of suggested Bible verses for Leroy to read. About a week later the story took an unusual turn when Paul received a telephone call from a woman who identified herself as Leroy's sister.

"I wanted to thank you for sharing the Lord with my brother," she told Paul. "My mother and I are Christians and have been praying for Leroy for many years. Until you prayed with him last week, he had always resisted the gospel."

Elated, Paul thanked her for the call, then out of curiosity asked her how she had gotten his number.

"I'm at Leroy's apartment right now. I found his Bible open on his desk with some Scriptures underlined in it, along with the note you sent him. But Paul," her voice trembled as she continued, "I also called to tell you that Leroy is dead."

Leroy is dead. The words extinguished Paul's euphoria like water thrown on a fire. He couldn't believe what he had just heard. Suddenly, his face felt flushed.

After taking a deep breath to regain her composure, Leroy's sister explained that he had been killed in a water-skiing accident the previous weekend. She concluded with the words, "I wanted you to know that because you were faithful to obey God, my brother is now with the Lord in Heaven. Your obedience made a difference in his life. Thank you."

Her words hit home. *"Leroy is dead...he's in Heaven...your obedience made a difference."*

The sun had set early for this young man so full of ambition and dreams. *Thank God we shared with him*, Paul thought.

Paul was still in shock when he phoned me with the news. Afterward, I sat quietly in my room, alone with my thoughts: *What would have happened to Leroy if I hadn't obeyed the simple prompting of the Holy Spirit? Where would he be right now? I almost blew it! How many other "Leroys" have there been in my life? How many opportunities have I already missed?*

I had come very close to allowing selfishness and fear to prevent me from being available for God to use in helping to lead a lost child back to Him. This extremely sobering experience made it crystal-clear to me that *every moment* counts! *This is not a game, but a war.* **It's a matter of life and death:** *eternal* life and death.

Seven Keys to Extraordinary Living

This experience with Leroy taught me several important lessons related to extraordinary Christian living. These lessons form the framework for everything that follows in this book.

1. Evangelism is a divine imperative.

As believers, we have a *divine imperative* to share the message of salvation with those who are lost. Remember the words of Jesus:

> *Therefore go and make disciples of all nations, baptizing them in the name of the Father and of the Son and of the Holy Spirit, and teaching them to obey everything I have commanded you. And surely I am with you always, to the very end of the age* (Matthew 28:19-20).

Note that this is not a suggestion, but an *imperative*. God has created *all of us* for lives of faith and power in Him and has called us to the ministry and mission of transforming our world with the gospel of Jesus Christ. It is a responsibility and a privilege that we all share together. The apostle Paul wrote:

> *...God...reconciled us to Himself through Christ and* **gave us the ministry of reconciliation**: *that God was reconciling the world to himself in Christ....And He has* **committed to us the message of reconciliation** (2 Corinthians 5:18-19).

The Lord wants to release extraordinary power *in* you to reach out to the world *around* you.

2. *Personal transformation is a must.*

Before we can be effective in transforming our world, however, we must first be transformed ourselves. Far too many Christians today, whether from selfishness, fear, lack of discipline, or ignorance, fail to claim their true heritage in Christ or realize what lives of power and effectiveness are available to them.

The key to extraordinary power in the life of faith is not *ability*, but *availability*. God uses people who make themselves available to Him. I almost missed a divine opportunity with Leroy because of selfishness and fear in my life. When we make ourselves available to God, He not only uses us in His work, but He helps us to conquer selfishness, laziness, fear, and other paralyzing obstacles in our lives.

We must become conformed to the image and likeness of Christ:

- Through the transforming of our *hearts*, "...having our hearts sprinkled to cleanse us from a guilty conscience..." (Heb. 10:22).
- Through the transforming of our *minds*: "Do not conform any longer to the pattern of this world, but be transformed by the renewing of your mind" (Rom. 12:2a).

In writing to the Corinthians Paul said that we should "take captive every thought to make it obedient to Christ" (2 Cor. 10:5b), and that "we have the mind of Christ" (1 Cor 2:16b).

God has released extraordinary power to begin, continue, and complete this transformation in you!

3. God uses ordinary people for extraordinary purposes.

The Lord's promise in Acts is for *every* believer:

> *But you will receive power when the Holy Spirit comes on you; and you will be My witnesses in Jerusalem, and in all Judea and Samaria, and to the ends of the earth* (Acts 1:8).

As we are being transformed in our hearts and minds, the Lord will use us to reach our "Jerusalem" (our family and friends) and, ultimately, the whole world.

This does not require extraordinary people or "super-saints." The believers in the New Testament were ordinary men and women who were totally committed to an extraordinary God, and they turned their world upside down. The same can be true today. God has always used the ordinary, the weak, and the simple to accomplish His purposes:

> *Brothers, think of what you were when you were called. Not many of you were wise by human standards; not many were influential; not many were of noble birth. But God chose the foolish things of the world to shame the wise; God chose the weak things of the world to shame the strong. He chose the lowly things of this world and the despised things—and the things that are not—to nullify the things that are, so that no one may boast before Him* (1 Corinthians 1:26-29).

Are you ordinary? Then you qualify! You *can* live an extraordinary life!

4. God has a sovereign plan for each of us.

The prophet Jeremiah wrote:

"For I know the plans I have for you," declares the Lord, "plans to prosper you and not to harm you, plans to give you hope and a future. Then you will call upon Me and come and pray to Me, and I will listen to you. You will seek Me and find Me when you seek Me with all your heart" (Jeremiah 29:11-13).

God's plan for you is different from His plan for me, but He has one for each of us. I had no idea what God had in store that evening when Leroy came to visit. A seemingly normal evening work shift turned out to have eternal significance. It was part of God's sovereign plan in Leroy's life. God had lined up all the parts of an intricate puzzle of which Paul and I happened to be key pieces. What a marvelous promise and encouragement these verses provide! What a privilege it is to participate in God's unfolding plan for this world. How do we learn God's plan for our lives? God stands ready to reveal His will if we will call upon Him and pray to Him and seek Him with all our hearts. James, in his Epistle, gives additional encouragement:

If any of you lacks wisdom, he should ask God, who gives generously to all without finding fault, and it will be given to him (James 1:5).

Extraordinary living involves discovering God's sovereign plan for your life.

5. Prayer unlocks the power for extraordinary living.

Prayer is our source of power, and is necessary for receiving daily "marching orders" from the Lord. Just before He ascended to Heaven, Jesus instructed His followers to "stay in the city until you have been clothed with power from on high" (Lk. 24:49). He also said to them:

*But you will receive power when the Holy Spirit comes
on you; and you will be My witnesses in Jerusalem, and
in all Judea and Samaria, and to the ends of the earth*
(Acts 1:8).

Jesus ascended to Heaven and the Holy Spirit descended
upon the believers ten days later on the day of Pentecost. What
did they do in the meantime? Luke tells us that "they stayed
continually at the temple, praising God" (Lk. 24:53), and that
"they all joined together constantly in prayer" (Acts 1:14a).
Holy Spirit power for extraordinary living came upon those
earliest believers in fulfillment of the Lord's promise, but it
also came after they had devoted ten days to continual prayer
and praise!

God is faithful to answer our prayers for loved ones.
Leroy's salvation was a direct result of the loving and consistent prayers of his mother and sister. Jesus said, "If you
believe, you will receive whatever you ask for in prayer" (Mt.
21:22), and "Ask and it will be given to you; seek and you will
find; knock and the door will be opened to you" (Mt. 7:7).
James wrote, "The prayer of a righteous man is powerful and
effective" (Jas. 5:16b).

As we learn how to *hear* and *discern* God's voice consistently, and obey, we will see His power at work in our lives,
and we will see our families and friends come to Christ!

6. Supernatural gifts equip us for extraordinary living.

Finding, developing, and using our supernatural gifts
enable us to live and walk in the supernatural realm, which is
crucial to our success. Hearing the voice of the Holy Spirit
unlocks the door to operating in spiritual gifts, which
empowers us to do the works of Jesus. The writer of Hebrews
referred to "gifts of the Holy Spirit distributed according to
His will" (Heb. 2:4b). Paul wrote to the Romans, "We have
different gifts, according to the grace given us" (Rom. 12:6a).

Discovering and using our spiritual gifts involves learning to listen to and walk in the Spirit:

> *So I say, live by the Spirit, and you will not gratify the desires of the sinful nature. ...Since we live by the Spirit, let us keep in step with the Spirit* (Galatians 5:16,25).

I listened to the Holy Spirit and subsequently shared with Leroy. The extraordinary gifts in you have that same potential! You will discover that God will use you in ways you had never dreamed possible!

7. Time is of the essence.

The time is now! There is an urgency as never before to reach our world with the gospel. Second Corinthians 6:2b says, *"Now* is the time of God's favor, *now* is the day of salvation."* Leroy's case shows how critical it is for us to act now. People are perishing around us daily. What will the Church do about it? As God's people, we must develop the *passion, conviction*, and *urgency* to radically obey Him *every* day, beginning *this* day!

Do you want to become a world-changer for Jesus? There is nothing more exhilarating in life than being a part of God's plan. I want to challenge you as you've never been challenged before. Ministry is not reserved for a few gifted individuals or pastors. If you have the desire, there is no reason why God cannot or will not use you! Are you ready to get started? Are you ready to participate with the sovereign Creator of the universe? Good!

Then let's get out of our spectators' seats and into the arena!

Chapter Two

Here I Am, Lord, Use Me!

Then I heard the voice of the Lord saying, "Whom shall I send? And who will go for Us?" And I said, "Here am I, send me!" (Isaiah 6:8)

"The success of our service in God is not dependent on our ability, but rather our availability."

—Smith Wigglesworth, *The Secret of His Power*

The loud squawk of the police radio interrupted my cup of coffee and donut.

"Three John One, please respond to the family fight in progress at 1053 Palace Drive."

"Ten-four," I responded, trying not to spill my coffee. *Family fights. Typical.* I was accustomed to these calls on weekend nights, when inevitably someone was drunk, loud, and belligerent. Often, weapons were involved. The worst part was seeing innocent children cowering and crying in the background. As I grumbled inwardly about the different possibilities, I suddenly remembered Jesus' words, "*Blessed are the peacemakers…*" (Mt. 5:9). I never liked these conflicts, but perhaps the Lord would use me as a peacemaker tonight.

It was a lower middle-class neighborhood of tightly-packed townhouses, which were surrounded by woods. I pulled up to one house, where a man was standing out front loudly pleading with the woman inside.

"C'mon! Let me in! I'm sorry! I'm sorry! I really am! I promise I won't ever do it again!"

The woman was screaming back at him through an open upstairs window. "Go away! I don't ever wanna see you again! You…"

When I went inside and spoke with the woman, she told me that the man outside, Dennis, was her ex-boyfriend who had regularly beaten her. Earlier in the day, she had sworn out a warrant for his arrest.

A "wanted" check confirmed that an arrest warrant had indeed been issued for Dennis. I placed him under arrest and handcuffed him with his hands behind his back. Then, in accordance with department procedure, I seat-belted him into the front passenger seat of my cruiser. On the way to the police station, the Holy Spirit began stirring my heart to share with Dennis. *No problem*, I grinned to myself. *I've got a "captive audience."*

While stopped at a traffic signal, I looked at him and asked, "Dennis, why *did* you hit your girlfriend?"

He looked down and became very quiet for a moment, obviously troubled by my question.

"You know, officer, I don't really know.…" His voice trailed off, then he continued. "If I drink a little too much and we argue.…" His eyes misted. "You know what happens. I can't believe the mess I've made of things. I know it's wrong, but it happens over and over again."

"Have you ever asked God to help you?"

His eyes opened wide, as if he was wondering, *Is this a joke? Is God playing a trick on me?* Then he smiled.

"As a matter of fact, I began attending a church last month, and it's really helped me."

After sharing my personal testimony with Dennis, I felt impressed to ask him if he knew about the Holy Spirit.

"I can't believe that I'm talking to a cop about all of this," he laughed. "I've been praying for the last month for the baptism in the Spirit, but for some reason I'm just not receiving. So here I am, sitting in a police car under arrest, and the cop is talking to me about the Holy Ghost."

"Maybe the Lord's trying to get your attention," I said.

At the police station, I needed an hour or so for report filing, fingerprinting, and mug shots. After that, I had to take Dennis to another city nearby to see the county commissioner, who would make the formal charges and set bail.

When we were halfway there, I received another impression from the Lord.

"Dennis, would you like to receive the baptism in the Holy Spirit right now?"

"You mean right here in the police car?"

"Sure, why not?"

Nervous, yet excited because of what I felt the Lord wanted to do, I pulled over to the side of the road and removed Dennis' handcuffs. As a police officer, I knew it was risky to take the handcuffs off of a prisoner in my custody, but I felt it was necessary. Dennis needed to know that I trusted him. How could he trust me if I didn't trust him?

Dennis had many questions, so we talked until he better understood God's mercy and grace. Then, I laid my hand upon his head, and we cried out to God for His wonderful gift. Suddenly, Dennis began to weep and shake uncontrollably. *Wow! I've never seen this before*, I thought. *This is powerful. It really works!* It wasn't sorrow or sadness that Dennis was experiencing. It was release—from years of loneliness, depression, and pain; from seeking refuge in a bottle and from rage that had kept him a prisoner and threatened to destroy every relationship that he had. Pure joy flooded over him as he laughed, cried, sang a little, then cried some more. He was completely overwhelmed by the presence and love of God in, of all places, a police car! It was as though invisible waves from the throne of grace were rolling in upon him to heal, restore, and empower him for service. (This was 1983, long before anyone had ever heard of the "Toronto Blessing"!)

Dennis continued to manifest God's presence even as we faced the stern-looking commissioner. At times he wept uncontrollably as the commissioner tried to advise him of his constitutional rights. Eventually, Dennis spoke up between his sobs.

"You probably think I'm weeping right now because I'm under arrest and in this situation, but that's not true. I'm weeping with joy because my Lord and Savior Jesus Christ has just baptized me with His precious Holy Spirit!"

The commissioner gave him an incredulous look, shook his head, and continued on with the proceeding.

Dennis was released on a personal bond (a signature) until his court date, then was free to go. As we drove back to the original scene of the crime we worshiped together to a Keith Green tape—brothers in Christ, a white man and a black man, a cop and a prisoner, worshiping Jesus together! My brother was filled, healed, and set free in his spirit that night, and oh, how my heart was filled with joy!

Dennis and I stayed in touch for the next four years. He returned to his church a new man, and he eventually became a leader there. Through this encounter, God restored a man's life and taught me something extremely valuable in the process.

Dennis and I spoke just recently, and he told me that he is now a licensed pastor. He said, "Erik, that night in the police car was the turning point in my life. Literally hundreds of people have come to Jesus since that night, as I share that testimony everywhere I go! Hallelujah!"

Available for Service

God will use us when we make ourselves available. It's not our *ability* that matters so much as our *availability*. We should be ready for God to use us anytime, anywhere, and in any situation.

Where Dennis was concerned, I could justifiably have reasoned to myself: *You have no business praying for a prisoner in your police car. What if something happens? What if he escapes, or even worse, takes your gun and shoots you?*

Often the fear of man causes us to miss the Spirit's prompting. I could have "wimped out" that evening. No one likes rejection. I certainly don't. No one likes to be embarrassed either, and few people enjoy being inconvenienced.

In the last chapter, I shared how I had struggled with selfishness and fear. Those sinful attitudes almost prevented me from leading Leroy to the Lord shortly before his death. I wish I could say that my struggle with those attitudes is over, but it isn't. It is a daily battle. I've noticed that often, just before God means to use us in a mighty way, the devil will oppose us strongly in the thought realm, bringing fear, selfishness, or apathy into our minds in an attempt to render us useless. The magnitude of the satanic attack against us is often proportional to the extent of the spiritual victory we could have by obeying God!

Serving God is not always convenient. In fact, it usually isn't. Jesus didn't say to us, "Follow Me when it's convenient, or when you feel especially motivated." Rather, He told us, "If anyone would come after Me, he must deny himself and take up his cross and follow Me" (Mk. 8:34b). The cross represents death: to self, to reputation, to convenience. However, Jesus also said, "My yoke is easy and My burden is light" (Mt. 11:30). When we follow Jesus with an abandonment of heart, He gives us the grace, desire, and motivation to do great things for Him. It can actually seem easy at times!

Availability to God means living our lives in complete surrender to Him, motivated by our love for Him. Jesus left no doubt about this when a Pharisee asked Him which commandment was the greatest:

Jesus replied: " 'Love the Lord your God with all your heart and with all your soul and with all your mind.'

This is the first and greatest commandment. And the second is like it: 'Love your neighbor as yourself.' All the Law and the Prophets hang on these two commandments" (Matthew 22:37-40).

Someone who loves God with all his heart, soul, and mind will make himself available to God. Such a love is total commitment. Availability to God means abandonment to His will. This was Paul's attitude when he wrote, "For to me, *to live is Christ* and to die is gain" (Phil. 1:21), and "I have been crucified with Christ and *I no longer live*, but Christ lives in me. *The life I live in the body, I live by faith in the Son of God*, who loved me and gave Himself for me" (Gal. 2:20). Paul's life was not his own. He belonged exclusively to Christ. That same self-abandonment and total availability to God is for us an essential key to living extraordinary lives.

Because I am reserved and shy by nature, I don't particularly enjoy meeting strangers or striking up new conversations. Many years ago, however, I made a decision to obey God and to be sensitive to His voice.

My former pastor, author Larry Tomczak, once made a statement that has been a continual source of motivation for me:

"The world has not yet seen what God will do with and in and through the man whose heart is fully consecrated to Him."[1]

Still single at the time, I typed out that quote and taped it to my bathroom mirror to read every morning as I shaved. I later memorized it and prayed it back to the Lord in my devotions:

"Lord, I want to be a man who is totally consecrated to You. I want You to use me mightily today to impact my world. Your Word says that You will do exceedingly and abundantly more than I could ever ask, imagine, or think, according to Your great power that is at work in me. Thank You, Holy Spirit, that You are in me. Here I am, Lord, use me today!"

If you want God to use you, then adopt this same attitude of heart. Make yourself available to God today. Determine in your heart that no matter the circumstances, place, or time, you will be ready to hear and obey God's voice. Pray Romans 12:1 every morning as you begin a new day: "Lord, I offer myself to You today as a living sacrifice."

Diligence vs. Laziness

Many of us have lofty dreams and aspire to greatness. Why is it then that so few of us actually achieve our dreams? Quite often the difference between dreamers and achievers can be summed up in a single word—*laziness*. The Book of Proverbs gives us a vivid picture of the person who is ever craving, but never achieving:

> *The sluggard **craves** and gets nothing, but the desires of the **diligent** are fully satisfied* (Proverbs 13:4).

> *A sluggard **does not plow** in season; so at harvest time **he looks** but finds nothing* (Proverbs 20:4).

> *The sluggard says, "There is a lion outside!" or, "I will be murdered in the streets!"* (Proverbs 22:13)

> *As a door turns on its hinges, so a sluggard turns on his bed* (Proverbs 26:14).

The sluggard is always dreaming—always desiring, always craving—but never succeeding. This is not to say that dreams and visions are not important. On the contrary, they are vital if we are to accomplish anything of value. The sluggard's problem is that no matter how high and lofty his dreams, he lacks the diligence and discipline to fulfill them. He simply doesn't get the job done.

Perhaps by now you are feeling a stronger desire to see God work mightily in your life! Maybe you have begun to develop a vision of how powerful and fulfilling your life in Christ can and should be. If so, great! My question now to you is, "What will motivate you to work diligently toward fulfilling your vision?" The sluggard is always making excuses for his lack of action: "There's a lion in the streets!" or "They'll laugh me out of the office if I say that!" or "I'm not ready yet!" or "Pray for that sick person? What if he doesn't get healed and then sues me?"

Actually, all of us are motivated by something. The question is, what? The guy who says he's not disciplined enough to pray an hour a day, is the same guys who spends "disciplined" hours in front of the TV. "But you don't understand," he says, "I just don't have time for evangelism." He always seems to have time to flip on the game, though, or to go shopping or to "surf the Net."

The key to proper motivation is recognizing the nature of our relationship with God and identifying His plan for our lives. If we keep those things before us, we will find the motivation to diligently follow the course of action He sets for us. Everything depends on our relationship with Him. Paul recognized the importance of this relationship when he wrote to the Philippians:

> *But whatever was to my profit I now consider loss for the sake of Christ. What is more, I consider everything a loss compared to the surpassing greatness of knowing Christ Jesus my Lord, for whose sake I have lost all things. I consider them rubbish, that I may gain Christ and be found in Him, not having a righteousness of my own that comes from the law, but that which is through faith in Christ—the righteousness that comes from God and is by faith. I want to know Christ and the power of His resurrection and the fellowship of sharing in His*

sufferings, becoming like Him in His death, and so, somehow, to attain to the resurrection from the dead. Not that I have already obtained all this, or have already been made perfect, but I press on to take hold of that for which Christ Jesus took hold of me. Brothers, I do not consider myself yet to have taken hold of it. But one thing I do: Forgetting what is behind and straining toward what is ahead, I press on toward the goal to win the prize for which God has called me heavenward in Christ Jesus (Philippians 3:7-14).

Looking back on my life, I have discovered that the times of my greatest discouragement and lack of motivation coincide with times when I have lost touch with God. The reverse is also true, however. My greatest motivation has come during those times when the Lord has personally revealed His will to me. (More on this subject in Chapter Six.) If we want God to use us regularly, it's crucial that we stay motivated, set practical goals in pursuit of our vision, and be diligent in working toward our goals. Personally, I set what I call "Life Goals," "Four-Year Goals," "Yearly Goals," and "Three-Month Goals." (A copy of these is in Appendix A.) I stay on track in the different areas of my life by prayerfully setting goals and then monitoring them regularly.

Take some time in the near future to contemplate your dreams, your motivation level, and your practical goals.

- What are the dreams you have for your life? Write them down.
- What personal goals have you set in working towards those dreams? Be specific.
- What things hinder your motivation in reaching these goals? Eliminate them or cut back.
- What encourages your motivation level? Take these to the Lord in prayer, and He will motivate you afresh to reach for the sky!

Fear Hindrances

I almost disqualified myself from ministry because of the fear of man. Perhaps you have the same fear as well. Many of us do. I had to consciously decide to confront my fear before God could release me from its stranglehold on my life. Francis Anfuso, an evangelist, once told of how he overcame his fear of the dark. One night, deciding that enough was enough, he determined to confront and conquer his fear once and for all! So he went upstairs into a completely dark room, into an even darker closet, and reached his hand up into the deepest, darkest recesses of that closet. He confronted his fear and has been free ever since.

Another common fear for many of us is sharing our faith with others. For some of us there is nothing more terrifying. It is undoubtedly one of the most anxiety-producing activities that many of us could ever imagine. That was my greatest fear as a new believer. Fear of rejection and fear of man were so strong that I would get sick inside just thinking about it. Perhaps your fear is public speaking, or praying for someone to get healed. Maybe you have a prophetic gift, but become paralyzed in public.

Whatever form it takes, fear is a crippler. Fear is probably the single greatest obstacle to our making ourselves available to God. Somehow, we must address and overcome our fears if we are to be truly available and useful to God. The Bible gives us some direction in overcoming our fears. In his letter to the Romans, Paul writes:

Do not conform any longer to the pattern of this world, but be transformed by the renewing of your mind (Romans 12:2a).

I needed desperately to renew my mind to break free from the fear of man. I began by praying, memorizing, and repeating out loud Scripture verses that dealt with fear and boldness, such as these:

I sought the Lord, and He answered me; and He delivered me from all my fears (Psalm 34:4).

There is no fear in love, but perfect love drives out fear (1 John 4:18a).

For God did not give us a spirit of timidity [fear]*, but a spirit of power, of love and of self-discipline* (2 Timothy 1:7).

The righteous are as bold as a lion (Proverbs 28:1b).

I am not ashamed of the gospel, because it is the power of God for the salvation of everyone who believes... (Romans 1:16).

The more I meditated, memorized, prayed, and spoke out God's Word, the more my fear was transformed into life-giving faith! I was on my way to freedom, but I still needed to face my greatest fear.

Endnote

1. This is a variation of the statement made in 1867 by evangelist Henry Varley to the young Dwight L. Moody, which inspired Moody's own powerful international ministry as an evangelist. Varley's original statement was, "The world has yet to see what God will do for, and through, and in, and by the man who is fully consecrated to him." Moody's response was, "I will be that man." Dwight L. Moody, a former shoe salesman who was neither ordained nor trained as a preacher, made himself available to God, and God used him during the next three decades to bring a million people to Christ.

Chapter Three

Facing Our Fear

"It is not the critic who counts—not the man who points out how the strongman stumbles or where the doer of deeds could have done them better. The credit belongs to the man who is actually in the arena—whose face is marred by dust and sweat and blood—who strives valiantly—who errs and comes short again and again. Because there is no effort without error and shortcoming. But he who does actually strive to do the deeds—who knows the great enthusiasm, the great devotions—who spends himself in a worthy cause—who as the best knows in the end the splendor, the triumph of high achievement—and who at worst if he fails, at least fails while daring greatly. So his place will never be with those cold and timid souls who know neither victory nor defeat."

—T.L. Roosevelt, *The Strenuous Life*

Open-air preaching…the very thought simultaneously stirred up in me both excitement and terror. Inspired after reading numerous accounts of Charles Finney and George Whitefield preaching to the multitudes, I often imagined myself also preaching outdoors to large numbers of unbelievers. I can remember how, as a new believer, I would stroll across the campus of the University of Maryland envisioning crowds of thousands gathered to hear me preach. Part of this was wishful dreaming, but I also had an honest burden for my campus. I wanted God to use me to reach people for Jesus, and I felt that preaching was one way to do it. There was only one problem. The whole idea scared me to death!

It was during this time that I joined a discipleship group of men in my church who also shared this burden for the lost. Ché Ahn, a pastor in Covenant Life Church at that time, led the group. I thoroughly enjoyed the teaching and motivational books that we studied, but the announcement that Ché made one night totally unnerved me.

"Next week we will go out together and open-air preach. Come prepared to share your testimony publicly."

My body tensed up as I heard those words. As long as we were only reading about such things, I was fine. Now we were actually going to do it! That was a different thing entirely!

Many of us experience similar feelings of dread when faced with the reality of putting into practice something we have learned. It's easy to simply *read* about the heroics and sacrifices of others. When the time actually comes for us to *act* upon our faith, many of us simply find an excuse or "chicken out." I hope that this book will inspire you to attempt great things for God. Simply reading it will do you no good, however, if you don't respond with positive action. It will be a waste of time. The Bible teaches the importance of acting on what we know. James certainly made it clear when he wrote, "Do not merely listen to the word, and so deceive yourselves. *Do what it says*" (Jas. 1:22). Although James was referring specifically to God's divine Word, the principle applies to every area of our Christian lives. Later in the same letter, James says that *true* faith shows itself in *actions*:

> *In the same way, faith by itself, if it is not accompanied by action, is dead. But someone will say, "You have faith; I have deeds." Show me your faith without deeds, and I will show you my faith by what I do* (James 2:17-18).

I loved learning about mighty men of God and how they lived. I dreamed that someday I might possibly do some of the things that they did. However, as soon as I was faced with a genuine opportunity to attempt something new, I wanted to run in the opposite direction! I had two options: face my fear and overcome it, or make excuses why it was impossible for me to change. (*I'm not ready yet. I need to grow more in Christ first. I'm not an evangelist like Finney. Friendship evangelism is more effective anyway. They'll think I'm a fanatic. What will my parents think? I have to work that night.*)

Actually, I *was* scheduled to work that evening, but I arranged to take off four hours so that I could go with Ché and the others. I knew I couldn't put it off any longer. It was time to face my fear. I prayed, confessed God's Word, wrote out my testimony, and practiced sharing it in front of a mirror. Even after all that, I was still afraid!

Finally, the evening arrived, and we traveled to an area near Washington, D.C., that is thickly populated by Cambodian and Laotian refugees. Ché chose a street corner flanked by apartment buildings. He began the outreach by telling the people that we were going to sing and share some testimonies.

As my turn came to preach, my knees literally began to shake. Summoning all the courage that I could find, I spoke with a loud voice, "My name is Erik Tammaru, and I'm here to tell you that Jesus Christ is alive! He's changed my life, and He can change yours!"

It was probably the shortest testimony ever given, but *I had done it*! I had faced my fear and knew then that it would never stop me again! I *could* preach in public! I had done it once, and I knew I would be able to do it again! Afterward, that same evening, I had the privilege of leading a young Laotian woman to Christ through an interpreter. That experience changed my life.

Since that night in 1983, by God's grace, I've preached hundreds of times in the open air to thousands of people in many different nations! It all began by simply facing a fear.

What are *your* fears? Fear of *man*? Fear of *rejection*? Fear of *embarrassment*? Many people give up without ever trying because of their fear of failure. As Teddy Roosevelt said in the quote that opened this chapter,

> "It is not the critic who counts—not the man who points out how the strongman stumbles or where the doer of deeds could have done them better. The credit belongs to the man who is actually in the arena...*who at worst if he fails, at least fails while daring greatly*" (emphasis added).

I would rather try and fail than never to have tried at all. I couldn't go through life tortured by thoughts like, *I wonder...* or *if only I would have....*

We all battle fear in our lives from time to time. The good news is that we don't have to stay in bondage to it. When we decide to face and overcome our fears, God will meet us powerfully and set us free.

Five Steps to Freedom

I want to share with you five steps that can help you in overcoming fear in your life. These principles have worked in my life and in the lives of many of the folks that I have had the privilege to lead. Give it your best, and with God's help, I'm sure that you will be victorious!

1. Make a decision to confront your fear.

Fear cannot be conquered accidentally or with a half-hearted approach. Only a deliberate determination to confront your fear will work. Right now you can decide to change. The Holy Spirit is speaking to your heart even now as you read this. Just as you once made a decision to follow Christ, make another decision right now to face that area of fear that has been keeping you from attempting great things for God. Take heart in the promise of His strength:

Look to the Lord and His strength; seek His face always (Psalm 105:4).

God is our refuge and strength, an ever-present help in trouble. Therefore we will not fear, though the earth give way and the mountains fall into the heart of the sea, though its waters roar and foam and the mountains quake with their surging (Psalm 46:1-3).

Now that you've decided, write down your decision right away. Don't wait, and don't read any further until you have done it! Write it in your journal or on a piece of paper to place inside your Bible. Type it into your computer or write it in the space below! Whichever you choose, write it down now! The longer you put it off, the easier it will be to forget about it altogether! Now, place a date next to it. One day you'll look back and remember how on this day God began the process of setting you free!

_____

_____ Date _____

2. Tell someone else about your decision.

Anytime I make a decision to change in an area of my life, I try to tell someone about it. The reason is very simple: If I *don't* tell someone, it will probably never happen.

For example, a few years ago when I wanted to lose some weight, I decided to begin a very stringent and consistent exercise program and diet. I informed my wife and my pastor of my goals. They were my accountability and support group. I knew that they would help and encourage me in meeting my goals. In the same way, I was accountable to Ché and the rest of the discipleship group as I determined to face and conquer my fear of open-air preaching.

Tell someone you trust and respect about your decision. Make yourself accountable to that person and ask him to pray with you and for you concerning your decision. The writer of Ecclesiastes knew the value of accountability and support:

> *Two are better than one, because they have a good return for their work: If one falls down, his friend can help him up. But pity the man who falls and has no one to help him up! Also, if two lie down together, they will keep warm. But how can one keep warm alone? Though one may be overpowered, two can defend themselves. A cord of three strands is not quickly broken* (Ecclesiastes 4:9-12).

If you are really serious about change, don't try to go it alone. We all need the help and support of others.

3. Meditate on, memorize, pray, and confess Scriptures that deal with fear.

We saw in the last chapter some of the importance of God's Word in the renewing of our minds. One of the most effective ways to deal with fear is to transform it into faith.

I once heard a Bible teacher say that fear is faith in the wrong direction. We are essentially saying, "God, the devil is more powerful than You are." When we fear failure, we are expressing the belief that we will fail. Fear is the opposite of faith. It is belief pointed in the wrong direction. This teacher taught me something else that was very helpful. He said that if we have a large fear capacity, we also have a large faith capacity. We need only to re-direct our belief in the right direction!

My wife and I have seen this borne out in our oldest daughter, Stephanie. When she was born, the Lord impressed on us that she would be a woman of strong faith one day. So we gave her Faith as her middle name. However, since her birth in

1985, we have watched her struggle again and again with irrational fears. For example, when she was little, on routine doctor visits, we would have to carry her in kicking and screaming. We have not been discouraged over this because we know that she will be a woman of great faith. Satan is trying to pervert that faith into fear. When she was eight years old she struggled with overwhelming fear as she went to bed at night. It was abnormal. I began praying with her every night, but she didn't conquer that fear until she memorized the following Scripture:

> *For God did not give us a spirit of timidity* [fear],
> *but a spirit of power, of love and of self-discipline*
> (2 Timothy 1:7).

The Word of God transformed her fear into faith! I now see in my daughter a great capacity for faith. For example, when we were living in Vienna, Austria, she was able to make friends in a foreign country and learn to speak German fluently much faster than the rest of us. Her faith was at work! Now as a teenager, she has a heart for God! So if you battle with fear, take heart! It simply means that you also have a large capacity for faith.

How can we turn our fear into faith? In the same way Stephanie did: We can renew our minds with God's Word. We need to train our minds to think the way God thinks. Take the Scriptures from the previous chapter or locate other meaningful Scriptures with the help of a good concordance. Write or type them out and carry them with you wherever you go so that they are handy for review. Tape them to your refrigerator or bathroom mirror. Practice regularly saying them out loud. Memorize them and make them a part of your daily prayer routine. Studies have shown that you need to say something seven times a day, for seven days, before it is really "learned by heart."

One tool that has been exceptionally helpful to me is a tract written by Larry Tomczak entitled, "Biblical Confessions to Build Your Faith,"[1] containing hundreds of Scriptures broken down into eight different sections: *Who we are in Christ; Victory; Faith; Boldness; Health; Joy; Prosperity;* and *Destiny.* It was so valuable to me that I memorized the entire tract and for a year prayed through a different section every day of the week: on Monday, *Victory*; on Tuesday, *Boldness*; on Wednesday, *Faith* and so on. That year revolutionized my life and laid a faith foundation I still draw from years later.

In 1986, I led a team of college students to Daytona Beach, Florida, during the dreaded "Spring Break" week. Our heart was to preach the gospel on the beach to the thousands of high school and college students who went there only to indulge in the four "*S*'s"—*Sun, Surf, Suds* (beer), and *Sex.* Knowing that it would be a daily battle against fear to go to the "devil's doorstep" and talk about Jesus, I required every member of the team to memorize beforehand the Scriptures on boldness from Larry's tract. It wasn't optional. I wanted every member to really know God's Word regarding faith and boldness. In addition, every morning before hitting the beach, we spent one hour in prayer and worship. Part of that time was spent confessing to God the Scriptures we had memorized. This would involve taking a Scripture, turning it around, personalizing it, claiming it as a promise, and praying it back to God. These are some examples:

- *The fear of man brings a snare, but perfect love casts out fear* (Prov. 29:25; 1 Jn. 4:18).
- *I sought the Lord and He heard me and delivered me from all my fears* (Ps. 34:4).
- *I'm not ashamed of the gospel for it is the power of God* (Rom. 1:16).
- *I'm an ambassador for Jesus Christ* (2 Cor. 5:20).

- *I fear not, for God is with me; He will strengthen me; He will help me; He will uphold me with His victorious right hand* (Is. 41:10).
- *I received power when the Holy Spirit came upon me to be His witness* (Acts 1:8).
- *I am strong, God's Word abides in me, and I will overcome the evil one* (1 Jn. 2:14).
- *Greater is He that is in me, than he that is in the world* (1 Jn. 4:4).

We were fully prepared to "blitz the beach" for God! Every one of us was involved in personal evangelism, drama, and open-air preaching. In an imposing atmosphere that was antagonistic at times, all of us battled our fears and overcame! How? God's Word at work within us transformed our fear into faith. After a week at Daytona, we were thrilled to have helped lead over 50 teenagers into a personal relationship with Jesus Christ! One young woman from Michigan who received Christ summed up the impact of our trip with this statement:

"I had everything in life anyone could want, but I didn't have the peace and joy that I saw in your eyes and in your lives. You don't know how much it means to me that you came all the way down here to share Jesus with me. My life will never be the same. Thank you."

I'll tell you, *our* lives were never the same after we got God's Word into our hearts. Even today, before I preach or evangelize, I first confess and pray God's Word to prepare myself. It's like taking a high-potency faith vitamin every day!

If you haven't already, begin now getting God's Word into your heart. It will change your life!

4. Make an appointment to do what you've decided.

Someone once said, "If you aim at nothing, you will be sure to hit it!" That's an understatement. Now that you have decided to "go for it" and confront the fear in your life, it's very important to set some very clear and attainable goals for yourself.

Begin by getting out your Daytimer® calendar or pocket agenda in an attitude of prayer. If you don't have one, get one now. The pocket-sized computerized planners can also be practical. Whatever will work best for you, get it before reading any further.

Looking at your calendar now, prayerfully consider dates to accomplish your goals, then write them down. For example, by next month, how many Scriptures will you memorize or pray through daily? How long will you pray daily? When will you share with your family or co-workers about Jesus? What are your goals for six months from now? Make sure you set realistic goals for yourself: too low and you won't really be challenging yourself to change; too high and you may fail and quit in discouragement. It's important to remember to trust the Lord also for the working out of your plans and goals. Here too there are scriptural promises to encourage you:

In his heart a man plans his course, but the Lord determines his steps (Proverbs 16:9).

Commit to the Lord whatever you do, and your plans will succeed (Proverbs 16:3).

Finally, set a specific date to confront your fear. Whether it is sharing your faith, preaching in the open air, or even starting your own business: whatever your fear, set a date to face it. Let God transform your fear into faith. Make an appointment now and prepare yourself for it. Otherwise it will never happen.

5. Find someone to go with you as a moral support.

Jesus knew the importance of moral support. In Mark 6:7 we read:

Calling the Twelve to Him, He sent them out two by two and gave them authority....

I have found it to be of immense value to bring along a support person to help in overcoming the fear of man.

Shortly after my brief open-air preaching episode with Ché I knew I needed to "get back on the horse" right away, so to speak. I wanted to try preaching to my peers at the University of Maryland, just as I had envisioned. It's one thing to go to a refugee neighborhood where no one knows you, but a different thing altogether when you are among acquaintances and friends. Knowing that I would never have the courage to attempt it alone, I called another one of my pastors at the time, Chip Ward, and asked him to accompany me for moral support. As it turned out, I really needed his encouragement.

One day at noon we went together to the Student Union Building of the College Park campus. After a few minutes of prayer, Chip had to literally push me out onto the sidewalk in front of the building. I preached for about ten minutes, then Chip followed me. Hundreds of people heard our messages. I never would have done it without Chip's moral support. Because of his support that first time, I was able to preach many times after that and later to develop a drama evangelism team that "preached" the gospel countless times all over the D.C. area. Once you "break through" that fear barrier, the sky is the limit!

Once you have set your goals, talk to a trusted friend, your spouse, or your pastor, and tell that person what you would like to do. Ask him or her to pray with you and hold you accountable to work toward your goals. See if your accountability partner will accompany you as you step out in faith. If you will follow these steps, trusting God in faith, the fear in your life will vanish, and in its place will be a new, bolder, and more courageous you! I guarantee it!

Endnote

1. You can order this tract by writing Larry Tomczak at 5123 Sherrer Drive, Acworth, Georgia, 30102.

Part Two

Transforming Our Minds

You will keep in perfect peace him whose mind is steadfast, because he trusts in You (Isaiah 26:3).

Do not conform any longer to the pattern of this world, but be transformed by the renewing of your mind. Then you will be able to test and approve what God's will is—His good, pleasing and perfect will (Romans 12:2).

Chapter Four

His Sovereign Direction

"God, from all eternity, did, by the most wise and holy counsel of His own will, freely, and unchangeably ordain whatsoever comes to pass."

—Chapter III, Westminster Confession

"If there is any part of creation that is outside of God's sovereignty, then God is simply not sovereign. If God is not sovereign, then God is not God."

—R.C. Sproul, *Chosen By God*[1]

Trust in the Lord with all your heart and lean not on your own understanding; in all your ways acknowledge Him, and He will make your paths straight (Proverbs 3:5-6).

Mmm...calzones, pizza, lasagna! They all looked and smelled so good. I was waiting in line at a pizzeria in the Harbor Place at Baltimore's Inner Harbor with one thing on my mind—deep-dish pizza with my name on it.

Out of the blue, a thought came rushing into my head: *Get ready, I have an assignment for you.*

This impression was so sudden and out of place that I recognized the Lord's signature on it. Making mental note of it, I proceeded with the purchase of what my father-in-law calls a "sartorial delight."

I returned to our table overlooking the harbor to enjoy the Sunday afternoon meal with my wife, children, and other family members. Having quickly consumed my pizza, I was leaning back in my chair to enjoy a cup of coffee when a woman walked past our table speaking loudly and excitedly.

"Eddie Murray is inside the restaurant!"

The all-star, switch-hitting, first baseman of the Baltimore Orioles was in the same building with us! An Orioles fan since my youth, this was a thrill for me. As soon as I heard this, I *knew* in my spirit that Eddie Murray was the assignment the Lord had prepared me for! I jumped up and grabbed my brother-in-law Keith for moral support.

"Come on!" I said to Keith. "I've got to share the gospel with Eddie Murray. That's what the Lord has told me to do."

With little enthusiasm, Keith replied, "Do you really think we ought to bother him?"

"Sure, why not?" Ignoring Keith's appeal, I went back inside the restaurant. Keith followed reluctantly. We searched for several minutes, but he was nowhere in sight. Dejected and disappointed, we returned to our table. I thought that somehow I must have missed God. I hadn't, though, for no sooner had we sat back down than Eddie Murray walked right past our table! He had three friends with him and they were all wearing sunglasses, trying to be "incognito." With my heart beating wildly, I got up and hurried over to them.

"Excuse me, are you Eddie Murray?" I couldn't hide the excitement in my voice.

Thinking that I was an autograph hound, he answered me rather curtly.

"No, man. You've got the wrong guy."

I was not willing to give up. "Are you sure you're not Eddie Murray?"

There was pleading in his voice as he answered. "No, man! Please leave us alone! I'm just out on a date with some friends." At this point the Lord gave me some wisdom.

"I don't want your autograph, Mr. Murray. I just want to give *you* something."

"You want to give *me* something?"

"Yes, Mr. Murray. I'm a Christian, and I have got a little booklet here that I would like you to read. Would you please read this?" I handed him the tract.

Paging through it he smiled and said, "Well, sure, why not?"

"Thanks, Mr. Murray. Sorry to have disturbed you."

"No problem." He turned and went on his way. *Wow!* I thought. *Eddie Murray! That was set up by You, Lord! Please touch his heart with that tract!*

Eddie Murray's mood had totally changed when I told him that I was a Christian and had something to give him. It was a *"Two Question Test—Are You Going to Heaven?"* tract written by Francis Anfuso, which I had with me in my wallet. I normally carried tracts in my police car or in my wallet for just such occasions as this.

Coincidence or Providence?

Was this only a coincidence or was a sovereign God at work "directing my paths"? I believe with all my heart that God does have wonderful and marvelous things prepared in advance for us. The apostle Paul wrote:

> *For we are God's workmanship, created in Christ Jesus to do good works, **which God prepared in advance for us to do*** (Ephesians 2:10).

I believe that every one of us has what Larry Tomczak calls "divine appointments." In his book of the same title, Larry shares the true experience of a mutual friend of ours, Patrick Lowery:

"One day, as he was working on a house in the Beverly Hills area, he noticed a young woman who seemed to be having car trouble. She asked if he could help her, and Patrick climbed down from his ladder, raised the hood of her very flashy sports car, and tinkered with the battery until he was able to get the car to start.

"The young woman, grateful for his assistance, asked if she could give him some money. Or perhaps she could thank him by taking him out to lunch?

"Patrick, who knows a divine appointment when he sees one, chose the lunch.

"As they drove off to the restaurant, Patrick turned to speak to the woman. She was wearing some rather plain clothes, but the numerous rings, bracelets, and necklaces she wore, not to mention the car she was driving, seemed to indicate someone of considerable wealth.

" 'My name's Patrick,' he smiled. 'Patrick Lowery. What's your name?'

"The young lady glanced at him curiously. 'Are you kidding me?' she asked.

" 'No, my name really is Patrick Lowery,' he replied. 'Who are you?'

" 'You mean you don't recognize me? You don't know who I am?'

"Patrick was beginning to feel a little awkward. Should he recognize the young woman seated next to him? He searched his Hollywood memory banks. A movie star? Someone in a big television series? He just couldn't place her.

" 'No, I'm sorry. Who are you?'

" 'I'm Madonna!' she laughed.

" 'Oh,' said Patrick. 'Madonna who?'

"Poor Patrick! He was too out of touch with the rock music scene to realize he was riding in a car with the biggest recording star of the year. Fortunately, he was enough in touch with the Holy Spirit to share his testimony and give her his personal life story, written up in a tract. She didn't seem too interested. But Patrick knew God had arranged some very unusual circumstances to enable him to plant a seed that could be watered at a later date."[2]

Sovereign Plans

Extraordinary power for extraordinary living depends to a large degree on our sensitivity to God's sovereign plan working in our lives. Developing that sensitivity is part of what it means to have our minds transformed into the likeness of Christ.

Contrary to what we may do or think, God is not in Heaven biting His nails, nervous that His plans will fail. He is God! He is omniscient! He knows everything before it even happens. We serve a sovereign, omnipotent, and omniscient God. Remember the Scripture from Jeremiah that I referred to in Chapter One:

"For I know the plans I have for you," declares the Lord, "plans to prosper you and not to harm you, plans to give you hope and a future. Then you will call upon Me and come and pray to Me, and I will listen to you. You will seek Me and find Me when you seek Me with all your heart" (Jeremiah 29:11-13).

These verses say several important things. First, they make it plain that God has a sovereign plan for each of us. Second, God wants us to know His plans for us and is ready to reveal them. Third, knowing God's plans for us involves honest, earnest seeking on our part. As we draw near to God, He draws near to us (see Jas. 4:8) and reveals His will as we seek to follow Him.

I am constantly amazed when I think of how God plans and orchestrates our lives. In the first chapter, I shared how the Lord had orchestrated the events in Leroy's life. If I hadn't arrived at Paul's home at the precise time ordained by God, Leroy would have knocked on the door of an empty house. God had sovereignly arranged every detail in advance! He knew that Leroy had an appointment with death the following week. I had the chance to participate with God in His sovereign plans. However, I could have decided not to, and thereby missed out on a part of my future reward in Heaven.

Sovereign simply means that God is in control. He is answerable to no one but Himself; He is accountable to no one but Himself. There is nothing in the universe outside of His sovereign will or control. Within His sovereignty, however, there is room also for our free will. God sovereignly chose to give us a free will, and He will not violate it. In His infinite wisdom and knowledge, He foresaw our sin, but He still chose to reveal His great mercy and grace to us by sending His Son Jesus.

This brings up a second point regarding our knowing God's plans for us. In addition to *seeking* His will and plan, we must practice *submitting* ourselves freely to His leadership. Even when we know His will, we must still make the conscious choice to obey. It is important to develop the attitude of living each day under His conscious direction. I think this is what James had in mind when he wrote:

> *Now listen, you who say, "Today or tomorrow we will go to this or that city, spend a year there, carry on business and make money." Why, you do not even know what will happen tomorrow. What is your life? You are a mist that appears for a little while and then vanishes.*

> *Instead, you ought to say, "If it is the Lord's will, we will live and do this or that"* (James 4:13-15).

Proverbs 3:6 (KJV) says that if we acknowledge God in all our ways, He will direct our paths. One of the reasons Paul's ministry was so powerful and effective was because he understood this truth. Paul was *totally surrendered* to Christ and sought to know the Lord's will at every turn. He then obeyed without hesitation or compromise. In Acts chapter 16, Luke records a good example of Paul's following God's sovereign direction, and its results:

> *Paul and his companions traveled throughout the region of Phrygia and Galatia, having been kept by the Holy Spirit from preaching the word in the province of Asia. When they came to the border of Mysia, they tried to enter Bithynia, but the Spirit of Jesus would not allow them to. So they passed by Mysia and went down to Troas. During the night Paul had a vision of a man of Macedonia standing and begging him, "Come over to Macedonia and help us." After Paul had seen the vision, we got ready at once to leave for Macedonia, concluding that God had called us to preach the gospel to them. From Troas we put out to sea and sailed straight for Samothrace, and the next day on to Neapolis. From there we traveled to Philippi, a Roman colony and the leading city of that district of Macedonia. And we stayed there several days. On the Sabbath we went outside the city gate to the river, where we expected to find a place of prayer. We sat down and began to speak to the women who had gathered there. One of those listening was a woman named Lydia, a dealer in purple cloth from the city of Thyatira, who was a worshiper of God. The Lord opened her heart to respond to Paul's message. When she and the members of her household were baptized, she invited us*

to her home. "If you consider me a believer in the Lord," she said, "come and stay at my house." And she persuaded us (Acts 16:6-15).

Paul's obedience to the vision and leading of the Holy Spirit opened up a small harvest! We should take hope and be strengthened in our faith with the knowledge that God truly is in control. He has chosen us and given each of us a destiny and a purpose. We can live every day with the assurance that God is directing our footsteps, as well as those of our loved ones, and will keep on doing it. Paul wrote to the Philippians:

Being confident of this, that He who began a good work in you will carry it on to completion until the day of Christ Jesus (Philippians 1:6).

That's a great promise! He who started it is the same One who will finish the work in you! You only need to be willing.

Sovereign Destiny

God has an exciting destiny for you! He knew you in your mother's womb and knows all the days He has planned for you! Destiny, I believe, means pre-ordained. But your destiny depends partially on your complete submission to His will.

My own life has been strongly impacted by the biblical account of the life and destiny of Josiah, one of the kings of Judah. In First Kings 13, around the year 975 B.C., we read of King Jeroboam as he was about to make a sacrifice at Bethel:

By the word of the Lord a man of God came from Judah to Bethel, as Jeroboam was standing by the altar to make an offering. He cried out against the altar by the word of the Lord: "O altar, altar! This is what the Lord says: 'A son named Josiah will be born to the house of David. On you he will sacrifice the priests of the high places who now make offerings here, and human bones will be burned on you'" (1 Kings 13:1-2).

Many years passed. Kings of Israel and Judah came and went. Some were good; most were evil in God's sight. The northern kingdom of Israel continued to sin against God and eventually was led away into captivity by the Assyrians and disappeared to history. The southern kingdom of Judah was also led into wickedness by many unrighteous kings. Around the year 649 B.C., a son was born to wicked King Amon and, upon his father's death, became king of Judah at the ripe old age of eight. His name was *Josiah.*

Eighteen years into Josiah's reign, during a renovation project to repair the temple, an amazing discovery was made there—the Book of the Law was found. It had been lost for many years and unknown to most of the people. As the Book of the Law of Moses was read aloud to Josiah, he was convicted of sin, tore his robes, and repented for the sins of Judah. He then began a vigorous campaign to restore righteousness in the land and destroy all forms of idolatry. In Second Kings we read:

> *Even the altar at Bethel, the high place made by Jeroboam son of Nebat...even that altar and high place he demolished....Then Josiah looked around, and when he saw the tombs that were there on the hillside, he had the bones removed from them and burned on the altar....The king asked, "What is that tombstone I see?" The men of the city said, "It marks the tomb of the man of God who came from Judah and pronounced against the altar of Bethel **the very things you have done to it**"* (2 Kings 23:15-17).

Can you imagine the emotions that must have washed over Josiah at that moment? He was a man of destiny. God had chosen him to bring a major renewal to the nation of Judah. *Over*

300 years earlier a prophet had come to the very place where Josiah was now standing and had declared, "A man named Josiah will come and bring desecration to this altar and spiritual restoration to his nation." That's powerful! God had a plan for Josiah's life, and it was being fulfilled! He might have rejected God's plan, but in humility, he committed himself to obeying God's will for his life.

In the same way, God has a plan for each of our lives! Do you really think it's a coincidence that you were born in the twentieth century? Think about it! More people are alive today than in the entire history of the world! We have a lost and dying world that is waiting for new "Josiahs" to come forth and fulfill their unique God-given destinies! Your life matters! Psalm 37:23 (NKJ) says, "The steps of a good man are ordered by the Lord, and He delights in his way." You can make an impact on the lives of countless individuals by and through your obedience to God. Your steps are certainly ordered by the Lord!

If we are to reach our potential in God, it's important that we understand His *daily* plans for us. We must also be prepared and alert for every "divine appointment" that He will bring our way!

Endnotes

1. R. C. Sproul, *Chosen By God* (Wheaton: Tyndale House Publishers, 1986), 26.

2. Larry Tomczak, *Divine Appointments* (Ann Arbor: Vine Books, Servant Publications, 1986), 57-58.

Chapter Five

His Sovereign Preparation

*...Always **be prepared** to give an answer to everyone who asks you to give the reason for the hope that you have...* (1 Peter 3:15).

*With this in mind, **be alert** and always keep on praying for all the saints* (Ephesians 6:18b).

Working the midnight shift as a police officer had its advantages and disadvantages. One advantage was that it was normally quiet during the wee hours of the morning during the winter. At least it was on my beat. Because of this, I took advantage of the quiet hours to pray, listen to teaching tapes, and memorize Scripture. This wasn't always the case, however. And one evening my peace and quiet was disrupted by a routine call.

"Three King Three," the dispatcher called, "please respond to the wine and cheese shop at Route 28 and Bauer Drive for a silent alarm."

"Ten-four."

I was off to check on a burglar alarm. We normally received as many as 20-30 false alarms every night in my district alone.

Just another false alarm, I thought, as I drove to the wine and cheese shop. *I wish these people would get their alarms fixed.*

I had already responded to hundreds of false alarms during my short time as a police officer. As a rookie, I had always followed the book and very carefully approached every alarm situation with extreme caution. For example, two patrol cars were always dispatched to an alarm. We were instructed to wait for our "backup" to arrive before we checked the premises. However, after a few years on the force with nothing but false alarms on these kinds of calls, it had become easy for me to let my guard down. Frequently, as the first officer on the scene, I checked things out alone and radioed in to "clear" the call. I wasn't being as alert as I should have been. I was getting too comfortable.

As I was driving to the wine and cheese shop on this particular night, I received a strong warning in my spirit to use extra caution. An overwhelming sense of danger came over me. I had what my wife calls the "heebie-jeebies."

In response to this warning, I decided to wait for my backup. When he arrived, I got out of my cruiser and walked very slowly to the rear of the building. I felt such a sense of foreboding that I removed my revolver from its holster and held it in the low-ready position—something that I rarely did.

We circled the building, checking all the entrance doors. They were "tight and secure." We shined our flashlights through the front windows. Seeing nothing, we cleared the call as a false alarm and went back on patrol. I was puzzled, but surmised that perhaps too much 7-Eleven coffee had given me the jitters. Never before on the job had I experienced such a strong feeling of danger.

The next evening, just before roll call, I was greeted by my sergeant.

"Tammaru! Come into my office."

"Yes, sir," I replied. "Is there a problem?"

"Why don't you tell me about that call at the wine and cheese shop last night." He looked like a disappointed father about to punish his son.

I explained to him what we had done. Giving me a stern look, he took a deep breath and said, "Last night the wine and cheese shop was burglarized. The burglars cut a hole in the roof and were most likely in the store when you responded. They broke into the safe and got away with a considerable amount of money. Please be more careful and alert from now on when you respond to alarm calls. It could save your life."

My sergeant had gotten my attention, and I was thankful that the Holy Spirit had also gotten my attention the night before. Who knows what would've happened if I had rushed into the call carelessly? Three years earlier, an officer from our department had been shot and killed on a similar alarm call in which burglars had broken through the roof of a department store.

Spiritual Alertness

My point in this story is that we should always be alert, not only in the physical realm, but especially in the spiritual realm. We are in a spiritual war, and opportunities surround us daily where we can follow the leading of the Spirit and win battles for the Lord. Danger is very real also, because there are spiritual enemies all around us. They tempt us to sin and seek to divert us, distract us, and destroy our witness for Christ. So we must be alert at all times! The apostle Peter gives wise counsel here:

> *Be self-controlled and alert. Your enemy the devil prowls around like a roaring lion looking for someone to devour. Resist him, standing firm in the faith, because you know that your brothers throughout the world are undergoing the same kind of sufferings* (1 Peter 5:8-9).

To be "self-controlled" also means to be sober and to watch. Being "alert" also means being vigilant. We should be careful to stay and walk close to God every day, never letting our spiritual guard down and never giving place or opportunity to the devil. Peter says that we are to resist the devil by standing firm in our faith. Once again, as James says, the key to this is our relationship with God:

> **Submit** *yourselves, then,* **to God. Resist the devil,** *and he will flee from you.* **Come near to God** *and He will come near to you. Wash your hands, you sinners, and purify your hearts, you double-minded* (James 4:7-8).

We cannot resist the devil in our own strength or power. Only as we remain in a right relationship with God through prayer, Bible study, and walking daily in the Spirit and in the power of the risen Christ can we stand up to satan and see him flee from us.

When Jesus went into the Garden of Gethsemane the night before He was crucified, He asked Peter, James, and John to "keep watch with Me" (Mt. 26:38) as He went a little farther to pray. Sleep overcame them, however, and when Jesus returned He warned them, "Watch and pray so that you will not fall into temptation. The spirit is willing, but the body is weak" (Mt. 26:41). In spite of this, they fell asleep again. Jesus emerged from His prayer vigil in the garden strengthened and ready to face the ordeal of the cross. His drowsy disciples, on the other hand, were unaware of the depth and power of the spiritual darkness around them, and due to prayerlessness, they were ill-equipped to face it and were caught totally unprepared by what happened that night. In fear of their lives, they fled into hiding, despite their brash promises to stay by Jesus' side.

Spiritual Armor

Jesus' disciples failed their first test of faithfulness under pressure because they were not spiritually prepared to do battle with the powers of darkness. Only later, after they were empowered by the Holy Spirit and were led by Him into a greater understanding of the truth, did the disciples avail themselves of the spiritual weapons that the Lord provided. In the garden, Jesus asked them to "stay" and watch with Him, but they did not. Just before His ascension, Jesus told them to "stay" in the city and wait for spiritual power from on high. This time the disciples obeyed, spending ten days in worship and prayer until the Spirit came upon them on the day of Pentecost.

Now, as then, a great spiritual war rages. The same weapons that the earliest believers had are available to equip us as well. Probably the best description of a Christian's preparation for spiritual warfare comes from the apostle Paul:

> *Finally, be strong in the Lord and in His mighty power. Put on the full armor of God so that you can take your stand against the devil's schemes. For our struggle is not against flesh and blood, but against the rulers, against the authorities, against the powers of this dark world and against the spiritual forces of evil in the heavenly realms. Therefore put on the full armor of God, so that when the day of evil comes, you may be able to stand your ground, and after you have done everything, to stand. Stand firm then, with the belt of truth buckled around your waist, with the breastplate of righteousness in place, and with your feet fitted with the readiness that comes from the gospel of peace. In addition to all this, take up the shield of faith, with which you can extinguish all the flaming arrows of the evil one. Take the helmet of salvation and the sword of the Spirit, which is the word of God. And pray in the Spirit on all occasions with all kinds of prayers and requests. With this in mind, be alert and always keep on praying for all the saints* (Ephesians 6:10-18).

We are to be spiritually alert at all times, but God doesn't leave us to our own devices. Take heart! Look at the arsenal of weapons that He has given us, both defensive and offensive: truth, righteousness, the message of the gospel of peace, faith, salvation, the Word of God, and prayer! This is not special equipment reserved for a select group of spiritually elite "supersaints," but standard issue equipment for every believer, for all the "ordinary" Christians like you and me. Just as every police officer receives a bulletproof vest, night stick, and revolver as standard issue (which are not to be left at home, but used daily), so *every* believer receives his armor that is to be used *daily*!

Spiritual Preparedness

It's so easy to go through our daily routines in a spiritual fog and forget all about the unseen world that surrounds us. I think that we would all act differently if we truly thought seriously about the invisible world. Think about this for a moment: There are angels around us every day looking over our shoulders! Most likely, there is one near you right now! These angels have been sent to help, serve, and protect us. Wouldn't you think twice about committing secret sins if you saw the angels all around you? I know I would. The Kingdom of God and the invisible world are just as real as the world we can see with our natural eyes.

Consider the fact that the Holy Spirit lives in us, ready and willing to give us supernatural direction and strength for daily living. How often do we grieve Him needlessly with sin, or frustrate Him with our inattentiveness to His voice. We should be spiritually alert and prepared for every opportunity that He will bring our way!

In the last chapter, I shared how a simple impression while buying some pizza prepared me for the chance to share the gospel with a celebrity. Let me say that everyone we share the gospel with is a celebrity in God's eyes, so who we share with is not important. We need to be alert for the impressions or promptings of the Holy Spirit. Divine appointments, whether with celebrities or with our neighbors next door, can be everyday experiences if we are alert and spiritually prepared.

Being prepared can also be as simple as always having a gospel tract with you. I didn't "just happen" to have a tract to give to Eddie Murray. I prepared in advance. Something we encourage all our church members to do is to write their own testimony tract. My wife and I wrote a short two-page tract containing our personal testimonies and a photo of us to give to people that we meet. Resembling a thick business card, it fits nicely in a wallet or pocketbook, and it is always handy for a "divine appointment." Today, with personal computers and color printers available to more and more people, it is even easier to write and produce your own tract. No one has ever rejected my personal tract. The usual response is, "Oh, you wrote this? How nice!" Our testimonies are powerful tools! (Samples of our testimonies can be found in Appendix B.)

> *We overcame Satan, by the blood of the Lamb, by the word of our testimonies, and because we loved not our lives even unto death!* (Revelation 12:11, author's paraphrase)

"God-Incidences"

As a new believer, I had an intense desire to be used of God to reach people for Jesus. One fall evening I went for a walk in my neighborhood to spend some time in prayer. It was just starting to get dark as I came upon an elementary school. I went into the playground and sat down on the grass to pray. Behind the building, about 50 yards from where I was sitting, a group of teenagers had gathered to loiter and smoke. I began praying for them and soon felt from the Lord that I was supposed to share with them. That's when the negative thoughts flooded in: *They'll think you're a Jesus freak. They'll laugh in your face. Don't let them interrupt your time of prayer.*

I didn't know what to do, so I tossed up a Gideon-type prayer:

"Lord, if You want me to share with these teens, have them come over here to me."

Within a couple of minutes, two of the boys walked over to me. They were about 14 years old and looked rather rough.

"Hey, what are you doing over here, man?" asked one of the boys, exhaling the smoke from his cigarette.

"Actually," I said with a small grin, "I was just praying that if I was supposed to tell you guys about Jesus, that you would come over here to me. And here you are."

For the next 15 minutes I shared my testimony of how the Lord had delivered me from "sex, drugs, and rock-'n'-roll." I told them that God loved them and wanted to know them in a personal way. As I continued sharing, I suddenly realized that I was now surrounded by about 20 teenagers wanting to know about God, Jesus Christ, and the baptism in the Holy Spirit!

Imagine that! A new believer preaching to a group of hungry and interested young people on a weeknight behind an elementary school! I had never done anything like this before. What was I to do next? I decided to give an invitation to the teens to receive Jesus right there in that playground. When I asked them if they wanted to receive Jesus as their personal Lord and Savior, about 15 of them raised their hands and then prayed with me! It was a real miracle, not just for them, but also for me! I began to pray for them, and the Lord gave me personal words of knowledge for many of them! For example, the Lord showed me that one girl, who was only 13, was already in a sexual relationship. I prayed for her and challenged her to repent and allow God to give her the love that she was seeking. In tears she prayed with me.

Was this a coincidence? Was it just a fluke, or something that I made to happen? No! It was what I call a "God-incidence." I believe that if every Christian would turn on his or her "Holy Spirit cell-phone" and tune in daily to the Spirit's voice, these "God-incidences" would be a common occurrence. Many of us, however, are not in touch with God outside of our quiet times and worship on Sunday morning. If we would take only 30 minutes each day to talk through our neighborhoods and pray for revival, *and* ask God to use us personally to reach our neighborhoods, I am convinced that revival would come to our communities. I am also convinced that God would use us mightily in the process!

Jesus said that the endtimes would be preceded by world evangelization:

*And this gospel of the kingdom will be preached in the whole world as a testimony to all nations, **and then the end will come*** (Matthew 24:14).

The Church needs to get serious about this call to world evangelization. We need to become spiritually alert and prepared for this all-important task. It is our *call*, it is our *privilege*, and it is our *sovereign destiny*. It begins with God's sovereign call on each one of our lives. It begins with me, and it begins with you.

Chapter Six

His Sovereign Call

"Winners take chances.
Like everyone else, they fear failing,
but they refuse to let fear control them.
Winners don't give up.
When life gets tough, they hang in
until the going gets better....
Winners know they are not perfect.
They respect their weaknesses
while making the most of their strengths.
Winners fall, but they don't stay down.
They stubbornly refuse to let a fall
keep them from climbing...
Winners believe in the path they have chosen...
even when others can't see where they are going."

—Nancye Sims, *Winners Take Chances*[1]

An angel grabbed my arm! It was a Sunday morning at
North Coast Church in Cleveland, Ohio, and I was praying in
a back room before the meeting began. At the time, I was part
of the pastoral team led by Ken Roberts (the senior pastor),

and it was our custom to pray together before the Sunday services. On this particular Sunday in early December 1989, there were only six of us in the room when the Lord spoke to me through a powerful vision. I saw in my mind the different nations of Europe, represented by different pictures. For example, a field filled with red tulips represented Holland. I also saw different national flags. Then, the Lord spoke very clearly to me: *You are to go to Europe this year. Assemble an evangelism team and go.*

As I stood there praying, my eyes closed, I suddenly felt someone grab my left arm. Expecting to see one of the other pastors, I opened my eyes but was surprised to find no one there! The nearest person was 20 feet away! Immediately chills began to travel up and down my spine as I realized that the Lord was really trying to get my attention! I believe an angel had been sent to show me the significance of my call to Europe.

On to Romania

December, 1989, was right around the time that the Berlin Wall fell and many Communist nations in eastern Europe began to open up. In fact, shortly after I had this angelic experience, Romania went through revolution and her terrible dictator, Nicolae Ceaucescu, was ousted and killed. Through different circumstances and connections, we made plans to visit this country in fulfillment of the Lord's call to go to Europe.

In October, 1990, after many months of preparation, my wife Crissy and I led a team of singles from our church on a two-week mission trip to Romania. This trip literally changed my life, for the Lord gave me further direction and details concerning His sovereign call on my life. My eyes were opened as never before to the tremendous hunger and openness of a world desperate for the gospel. For the first time I really understood Jesus' words when He said, "I tell you, open your eyes and look at the fields! They are ripe for harvest" (Jn. 4:35b).

We flew into Vienna, Austria, where we met a wonderful man of God named Ilie Coroama, a Romanian-American who had miraculously escaped from the Ceaucescu regime in 1974. Ilie endured months of persecution, torture, and imprisonment before being literally led out of the country by a pillar of light that appeared to him and two other men! Eventually, he made his way to America where through a series of miracles, his wife and ten children were able to join him. Since the collapse of Communism in Romania, Ilie has been bringing God's love back to his homeland in the form of Bibles, food, medical supplies, and even building an orphanage. He was our contact point and companion for our two weeks in Romania.

Angelic Direction and Protection

In Vienna, we loaded three large vans with Bibles and other supplies for the Romanians. The long drive took us through Hungary, and we spent much of the time in worship and prayer. As we neared the Hungarian-Romanian border, I received a vision from the Lord of a man standing in the road pointing to the left. Even as I wondered what it meant, the Holy Spirit spoke to me, "This is an angel sent to guide you and protect you on your journey."

I shared this with everyone in our van, and we continued to pray. Shortly after this, we arrived at the border to find in front of us a line of cars and trucks extending for three to four miles, all waiting to enter the country. The line was not moving at all, and it appeared that we would be waiting for days to get in! What were we going to do? We were 20-some people crammed into three vans and on a tight schedule, knowing that the Lord had called us here to reach Romanians for Jesus. We couldn't afford to wait days to get into the country!

Thank God Ilie was with us! The man who had an anointing to escape from Romania certainly had an anointing to get into the country as well! Impulsively, he pulled his van into the oncoming lane of traffic and said, "Start praying!" We prayed as we moved slowly past the line of vehicles on our right. Whenever oncoming traffic came, somehow we squeezed through the middle. About 200-300 yards from the border, a uniformed soldier appeared from nowhere in the middle of the road. Stopping us, he came up to our van and spoke to Ilie.

"Where are you going?" he asked.

"We are Christians bringing Bibles and other things to help the poor people in Romania," Ilie answered softly. "Could you please help us?"

The soldier smiled, then, *pointing to the left*, said, "Go through that special entrance."

Our three vans pulled around to the left side and entered into a special place reserved for buses. We had bypassed hundreds of cars, and God sovereignly guided us into the country! After a short stop, we were on our way to Moldavia, Romania!

Was the soldier an angel sent to help us? I believe that he was. We gave out thousands of Bibles and gospel tracts during the ten days we were in Romania. We also ministered in many churches and visited the poor and orphans. It was not all smooth sailing, however. We were also hassled by gypsies, followed by the Securitate (the dreaded secret police), and received threats while we were there. Thank God an angel of the Lord was watching over us the entire time!

One significant result of our Romania trip was that, while we were there, the Lord called our family to the mission field. Crissy and I received a very clear word that we were to move to Vienna, Austria, and establish a base of ministry there to reach Europe with the gospel. Over the next two years we were to see that word tested many times.

Testings

When the Lord speaks a word to us, we need to be prepared for that word to be tested, and tested thoroughly. Usually, the bigger the word, the bigger the testing. It is during these times of testing that we learn to trust God, develop our faith, and see our sovereign God at work. I love this Scripture from Numbers:

> *God is not a man, that He should lie, nor a son of man, that He should change His mind. Does He speak and then not act? Does He promise and not fulfill?* (Numbers 23:19)

When God promises us something, He is faithful to perform it. Period. During the testing time, however, it can be difficult to see the end of the tunnel. During our two years of testing, we had to continually remind ourselves of God's goodness and faithfulness.

For one thing, we had to convince a lot of people that we were indeed hearing from God: our senior pastor, the leaders of the ministry that we were in, and our family and friends. A common response seemed to be: *"You want to do **what**?"* Another obstacle that was always raising its ugly head was the fear of failure. Many well-intentioned people gave us advice and raised issues of concern. These are some of the questions we faced:

- "How will you reach people from another culture and language?"
- "What about the finances?"
- "But the spiritual ground is so hard there."
- "Won't that be difficult for your children?"
- "Won't it be hard to leave your families and friends and your good job for something so risky?"
- "What if you fail?"

It was during this same time that I first read the poem by Nancye Sims cited at the beginning of this chapter:

> *"Winners take chances.*
> *Like everyone else, they fear failing,*

> *but they refuse to let fear control them.*
> *Winners don't give up.*
> *When life gets rough, they hang in*
> *until the going gets better....*
> *Winners fall, but they don't stay down.*
> *They stubbornly refuse to let a fall*
> *keep them from climbing...*
> **Winners believe in the path they have chosen...**
> **even when others can't see where they are going.***"*

I took much courage from those words. God was speaking encouragement and faith to me through that poem! Maybe no one else could see what I was seeing, but I had to at least have the courage to try and possibly fail. How many men and women of God have felt alone or wanted to quit after receiving a promise from God? How many folks, when confronted with the test, have quit when the naysayers came and pointed out how they would fail? Chuck Swindoll writes:

"Great accomplishments are often attempted but only occasionally reached. What is encouraging is that those who reach them are usually those who missed many times before. Failures, you see, are only temporary tests to prepare us for permanent triumphs."[2]

We shouldn't be afraid of failing! When Thomas Edison was asked about his hundreds of "failed" tests at making a light bulb function, he replied, "Those aren't failures! Rather, now I know a hundred ways that a light bulb won't function!" He wasn't afraid of failure! He also went on to invent the light bulb. When I visited his winter home in Ft. Myers, Florida, I saw some of his original light bulbs that are still in use today!

When times of testing come (and they will come), we need to trust God! It is a time to watch our God work in wonderful ways! During our two years of testing, we recorded so many confirmations of our call to missions that we had absolutely no doubt that we were doing the right thing.

Timing

One of the critical things to remember during times such as these is to trust God's timing. No matter how impossible or improbable the fulfillment of God's call may seem at any given moment, He will work everything out in His own time.

This very issue of timing is one point that is often given to people receiving counseling regarding a "word" they've received from God: "That's a good promise you've received, brother, but we'll have to wait to receive the Lord's timing on that one."

Certainly, there is wisdom in seeking God's timing, but sometimes while we are waiting around for the perfect timing, the opportunity can pass us by! Often, people making the above statement really mean: "That sounds a little too risky, so why don't you wait, pray, and fast, for say, ten years, and then we'll talk about it again!"

Hearing from God and trusting Him for a promise boils down to being willing to take some risks. Everything that involves faith involves risk. Take Peter, for example. He wanted to walk on the water. Seeing Jesus out there, his child-like faith said, "Hey, I want to do that!" He asked the Lord, "Can I try it?" Jesus said, "Come on!" There was a risk there. Peter could either sink or swim, so to speak (pun intended), or he could have waited: "Maybe I need more confirmation or clarity on the timing of this thing!" No! Peter took the risk, jumped out of the boat, and walked on the water!

Faith is all about taking risks! Sometimes it means burning your bridges behind you. That's what the prophet Elisha did. In First Kings chapter 19, Elisha received the call from Elijah to follow him. Realizing immediately the significance of this call on his life, as well as the risks involved, Elisha asked Elijah if he could at least say good-bye to his family. Then we read:

So Elisha left him and went back. He took his yoke of oxen and slaughtered them. He burned the plowing equipment to cook the meat and gave it to the people, and they ate. Then he set out to follow Elijah and became his attendant (1 Kings 19:21).

Talk about burning your bridges! Elisha didn't just take a "leave of absence from the 'firm'." He killed his oxen and burned his plow equipment. As far as he was concerned, his former profession was over! Then he held a farewell party to say good-bye to his family and friends. Elisha was a man who was committed to his call.

Proper timing is critical, and we need to be sensitive and patient to allow God to bring about His purposes. At the same time, however, we need to be alert to the possibility that risks may be a necessary part of those purposes. Sometimes, full confirmation comes only after we get out of the boat and take a risky step of faith.

Confirmations

As I was praying one evening during our time of waiting for the release to go to Europe, the Lord dropped this word into my spirit: *Your next child will be born in Austria.*

Pow! My first response was, "Lord, excuse me, what child? I thought we were finished!" We had four children already, and we were very content with the size of our family. Needless to say, this was somewhat of a shock. About two weeks later, my wife took a pregnancy test and found that indeed we were "with child"! The conception date lined up perfectly with the day God had spoken to me! Now we knew with great clarity that we were to be in Austria within nine months. God is good to bring confirmation and encouragement when He knows we need it.

The risk was becoming a reality. We sold our house and our car, held garage sales, and gave away a lot of things. We were burning our bridges. In June 1992, a little over two years after the Lord had told us to go, my four children, my very pregnant wife, and I boarded our airplane armed with 18 pieces of luggage—all our worldly possessions. Hours later, we arrived in Vienna, Austria, to begin our new lives as missionaries, following the sovereign call of God on our lives.

How about you? Are you following God's preordained and wonderful plan for your life? Or are you settling for a mediocre, mundane, or average existence? The choice is yours alone. Too many people settle for "the house with the picket fence" or "keeping up with the Joneses." There is so much more to life! We have the chance to build up treasures in Heaven and work toward eternal goals. The fact that you are reading this book shows that you desire to serve God and that you have a heart for the lost and for evangelism. What are you waiting for? Get moving! Find out God's plan for your life and invest yourself 100 percent. As a young Christian, I was deeply impacted by something the late Arthur Wallis said:

> "If you would serve God well with your life, find out what God is doing in your generation, *and fling yourself into it*."

Fling yourself into it! Give it a 100 percent commitment and go after your dreams! While I was in the testing time and waiting for the release to go into missions, I had a medical check-up that I'll never forget. I was finishing the EKG test and talking casually with the nurse, when she suddenly turned to me and said:

> "If I had one piece of advice to give to someone your age, it would be this: *Go after your dreams*. Do it now while you are still young. You'll never have the chance again."

The Lord was speaking through that nurse! If only she had known what I had been praying about for months! I would give you that same advice. Go after your dreams! Don't wait for them to come to you! As the famous shoe advertisement goes, "Just Do It!" If you're waiting for a call to evangelize, or to go into missions, wait no longer. Matthew 28:19 is all you need for confirmation:

Therefore go and make disciples of all nations....

So get moving! Go on a short-term mission trip. Take part on the evangelism team in your church. Get some training. Go back to school. Join the drama team. Start that business. Learn to play that musical instrument. Pray for the sick in church. Get your music group started. Some of you reading this book are called to the mission field. Prepare yourself. Learn that second or third language. Get started right away while the inspiration is there, and commit to the Lord all your plans in prayer. There is nothing more rewarding than following God's sovereign call in your life!

Endnotes

1. An excerpt from Nancye Sims, "Winners Take Chances." Copyright© Blue Mountain Arts, Inc. Taken from Vickie Mitchell, "Poet Shares Fame of Her Fan Half a World Away," Lexington Herald-Leader, August 27, 1997.

2. Chuck Swindoll, *The Grace Awakening* (Dallas: Word Books, 1996).

Part Three

Transforming Our "Jerusalem"

But you will receive power when the Holy Spirit comes on you; and you will be My witnesses in Jerusalem... (Acts 1:8)

"The Lord will do everything by prayer, and nothing without prayer."

—John Wesley

Chapter Seven

Answer the Phone!

"Every believer has the Holy Spirit in him to lead and guide him; each believer can hear from God for himself."

—Kenneth E. Hagin, *He Gave Gifts to Men*[1]

With lights flashing and siren wailing, cruiser 889 pursued the white pickup truck at high speed through the small town. The two young men in the truck were intoxicated and doing their best to elude me. I radioed in to the dispatcher my coordinates and direction of pursuit as I tried to catch the pickup. Suddenly, the driver turned into a neighborhood sub-division and turned off his lights. In the dark of the moonless night, the truck vanished. *Darn it! Where are they?* I thought in desperation. *You're not going to get away from me!* I began to pray, "Oh God, don't let them get away! Help me catch these guys!" I drove slowly through the sub-division, searching frantically with the cruiser's spotlight. After five minutes or so, I became totally frustrated and was ready to give up. Even now I could hear the ribbing that I would receive back at the station for losing a "DWI" (driving while intoxicated):

> "Hey, Tammaru, another drunk get away from you? Haw haw! Maybe you should take the training wheels off of your cruiser, Rookie!"

I groaned at the thought of it. Just as I was about to radio in that I had lost the driver, I heard a voice in my head: *Don't you trust Me? Didn't you ask for My help? Don't give up yet!*

The voice was so clear that I knew it was God. It gave me fresh hope that I would catch the drunk driver. As I drove around the next corner, my spotlight found something very interesting. Backed into a driveway with his lights out, the DWI was sitting in his pickup truck with a very surprised look on his face. The Lord had helped me find my man! After arresting and booking him, I later drove the young man home in my police car. I had a chance to share my testimony with him, and he prayed to receive Christ as his Lord and Savior right there in my cruiser. A few weeks later, he even attended our church. God had literally "arrested" this young man to get his attention!

Receiving Marching Orders

I've had many experiences similar to this one where, in the course of a day, the voice of the Lord broke in with a new assignment. If we are to be successful disciples of Jesus, we need to do what He did. A friend and co-laborer of mine, Jon Palmer, once made an astoundingly simple but truthful statement:

"If you want to do the things that Jesus did, then do the things that Jesus did."

In other words, if you want to do the miraculous things that Jesus did, such as healing the sick, working miracles, leading people to salvation, or casting out demons, then you need to first do the other things that Jesus did: praying, fasting, and *waiting daily* for God's instructions. Essentially, this means maintaining a living relationship with God. Speaking of His Father, Jesus was able to say, "I have completed the work [He] gave me to do" (see Jn. 17:4). I believe that Jesus knew exactly what He was supposed to do every day. As He spent those early morning hours in prayer, He was receiving His marching orders for the day. On another occasion, Jesus said:

...the Son can do nothing by Himself; He can do only what He sees His Father doing... (John 5:19).

Jesus was in touch with the Father and filled with the Holy Spirit without limit, yet even He needed to be in constant communication with His Father. That was the key to His ministry. In the same way, if we want to be used by God, how much *more* should we be in communication with Him. Jesus told us that we would be able to do even greater things than He did because He was sending us His Holy Spirit (see Jn. 14:12-17)! That's an incredible promise! We *can* do the things that Jesus did, but *we first need to do the things that Jesus did*! We must *daily* hear God's voice and receive our new instructions for the day.

Why are there not more Christians who are hearing God? I believe it is because their phones are off the hook, so to speak, or their lines are busy, or perhaps their phone lines are disconnected. Worse yet, perhaps their phone lines to the Father are not even installed!

My Romanian friend Ilie always says:

"Keep your phone lines busy with God! His telephone number is Jeremiah 33:3—*'Call to Me and I will answer you and tell you great and unsearchable things.'*"

Sounds simple, doesn't it? It is and it should be. Why, then, don't we do it?

Make an Appointment With God

Some Christians don't hear from God because they are never home when the telephone rings. There's no such thing as a spiritual answering machine, even though many people try:

"Lord, I'm not available right now. Please leave a message after the beep. When I can fit You into my schedule, I'll get my messages, and possibly even return Your call."

Sometimes they screen their calls and answer only when it's convenient or it's someone they want to talk to. Does this sound familiar?

"Hello, we're not home right now. Please leave a message after the beep...."

"Hey Erik, it's me, Jeff. Come on, pick up the phone! I know you're there. I wanted to know if you'd like to play golf...."

Immediately, I jump to get the phone when I hear something like this. Unfortunately, many of us try to do that with God; we only answer His calls when we think that it's something that we want to hear.

Can you imagine treating a king that way? What if the President of the United States called to speak with you? You'd pick up that phone in an instant! Second Corinthians 5:20 says that we are ambassadors for Christ, and the King of kings—the King of the universe—wants to make an appointment to speak with us every day. It's really amazing when you think about it. However, we must make time with God to hear His voice and receive His orders. Our Father in Heaven wants to communicate with us. As a natural father, I know that I can't wait for my kids to wake up so that I can hug them and tell them that I love them. I'll go into each room in the morning, and rub their heads or tickle their bellies and say, "Time to get up!" I look forward to that time. It's the same way with God. He can't wait to spend time with us and communicate His heart.

Find a time that works well for you and meet with your heavenly Father. Perhaps you are a morning person like my wife. If you are like me, on the other hand, and require a second cup of coffee before that second brain cell in your head comes to life, perhaps evenings are better. When I worked at the United Nations Headquarters in Vienna, Austria, I prayed daily as I jogged during my lunch hour in a park next to the complex. Find something that consistently works for you. I can't stress enough how important it is to have a regular "quiet time" with the Lord.

Once, when I was teaching a foundations class in my church here in Basel, Switzerland, I was talking about the importance of prayer and daily quiet times. Speaking in German, I made one of my many mistakes. I translated "quiet time" into *"Stillzeit."* The people laughed hilariously and told me that *"Stillzeit"* means to nurse a baby! I should have said, *"stille Zeit,"* which means "quiet time." As I thought on it later, however, I realized that I wasn't so far off base! Our daily times with God are like a baby being fed milk by its mother. We need the daily "milk" of God's Word for nourishment and comfort. We need to commune with our Father and daily receive His love. We are careful to feed our physical bodies every day, but our spiritual bodies need nourishment as well.

David, master psalmist and king of Israel, understood this very well. He enjoyed an intimate and rich fellowship with God, which showed up frequently in his psalms:

Be still before the Lord and wait patiently for Him; do not fret when men succeed in their ways, when they carry out their wicked schemes (Psalm 37:7).

I waited patiently for the Lord; He turned to me and heard my cry. He lifted me out of the slimy pit, out of the mud and mire; He set my feet on a rock and gave me a firm place to stand. He put a new song in my mouth, a hymn of praise to our God. Many will see and fear and put their trust in the Lord (Psalm 40:1-3).

*In the morning, O Lord, You hear my voice; in the morning I lay my requests before You and **wait in expectation*** (Psalm 5:3).

*Hear my voice when I call, O Lord; be merciful to me and answer me. My heart says of You, "Seek His face!" **Your face, Lord, I will seek*** (Psalm 27:7-8).

Wait for the Lord; be strong and take heart and wait for the Lord (Psalm 27:14).

***I wait for the Lord, my soul waits**, and in His word I put my hope. **My soul waits for the Lord** more than watchmen wait for the morning, more than watchmen wait for the morning* (Psalm 130:5-6).

Busy Signals

Others don't hear God because whenever He tries to call them, He gets a busy signal. These people are so busy talking or bringing their demands to God that they don't take the time to listen to Him. King Solomon, a man of godly wisdom, gives us this advice:

He who answers before listening—that is his folly and his shame (Proverbs 18:13).

Prayer is a two-way conversation. Can you imagine the frustration that my wife would feel if I never allowed her to speak when we met?

"Oh, Crissy, you are so beautiful and lovely. I love you so much. Thank you that you care for me and the children. By the way, could you iron my shirts? And could you take the car in for a servicing? And could you give me a new watch for my birthday? Oh thank you, my

wife, thank you, my treasured friend, thank you, my lover and the cooker of my meals! And..."

You get the idea! She would appreciate my praise and compliments, but she would also want to communicate with me! In the same way, God desires fellowship with us, His children. Our worship, thanksgiving, and praise are important—even essential—in our relationship with God, but sometimes we need to simply stop and listen and let God speak to us. Psalm 46:10 says, *"Be still, and know that I am God; I will be exalted among the nations, I will be exalted in the earth."* Many times, it is in our *stillness* before God that we really come to *know* Him, *hear* His voice, and *understand* His will.

That's the beauty of Christianity. We're not supposed to live out dry religious traditions, or a form of godliness. In Christ, we don't have a *religion*; we have a *relationship*! Jesus' death and resurrection reestablished the line of communication between God and His creation. We can know our God intimately and speak with Him as a friend. If we don't understand this, we are missing the entire point of Christianity—fellowship with God! Paul wrote to the Corinthians, "God, who has called you into *fellowship* with His Son Jesus Christ our Lord, is faithful" (1 Cor. 1:9). John wrote in his first letter, "We proclaim to you what we have seen and heard, so that you also may have fellowship with us. And *our fellowship is with the Father and with His Son, Jesus Christ"* (1 Jn. 1:3).

Allow the Lord to speak to you as you quiet your soul before Him in prayer. Don't do all the talking. Speak and *listen*. Spend time reading His Word—His love letter to us—and allow the Holy Spirit to highlight passages to you.

The Lord also desires to speak to us during the course of the day. I'm convinced that the Lord is always speaking. We just need to tune in and listen. Our lives are so busy and so preoccupied with daily problems and routines that we don't wait to listen for the gentle voice of the Spirit. How often do we make wrong decisions simply because we fail to ask God and then wait for an answer or impression from Him? We miss "divine appointments" as well because we are simply not in tune with God.

Phone Line Installation

There are others who do not hear God's voice because their line has been disconnected or was never installed in the first place. Paul told us,

> *...those who are led by the Spirit of God are sons of God* (Romans 8:14).

If you are a born-again believer in Jesus Christ, you are a child of God. As a child of God, you have God's Spirit living in you, but are you filled with the Holy Spirit to overflowing? The baptism in the Holy Spirit is the gateway to a life lived in the supernatural realm, and it is a key to hearing God's voice with ever-increasing clarity. After Pentecost the disciples of Jesus Christ were "filled" or "baptized" with power to become His effective witnesses (see Acts 1:8; 2:1-41). They plugged into the power source and were mightily used of God! If you want to hear the voice of God and be mightily used, get plugged into the "phone jack" and power source—the Holy Spirit! Jesus said that His Father would give the Holy Spirit to whoever asked Him, even as a human father will give his children food when they ask (see Lk. 11:10-13). With simple childlike faith, we can come to our perfect heavenly Father and ask Him to baptize us—immerse us—fill us—with His precious Holy Spirit! If you want this experience, you can ask God to fill you right now in the privacy of your room. Lift up your hands to Him and repeat this simple prayer:

> *"Heavenly Father, thank You that You sent Jesus to die for my sins. Thank You that when Jesus ascended into Heaven, He promised to send the Holy Spirit to indwell us and empower us. You said that we must only ask You*

for the Holy Spirit and You will fill us and baptize us with His power! I believe Your Word! I ask You, Jesus, right now to baptize me in the Holy Spirit. I want to be overwhelmed and filled with Your presence and peace. Come now, Holy Spirit, and take control. I praise You and thank You, Lord! I receive right now by faith, in Jesus' name! Amen!"

Now begin to thank Him and worship Him verbally (out loud!) as the Holy Spirit leads you. If you need more help, talk to your pastor or home group leader.

The baptism (filling) of the Holy Spirit is not just a one-time thing. Paul tells us in Ephesians, "Do not get drunk on wine, which leads to debauchery. Instead, be filled with the Spirit" (Eph. 5:18). The Greek word used here for "filled" is *pleroo*, which means to refill something after it has been emptied, to cram into, or to level off something that was hollow. As used in this verse, it refers to a *continuing action*—to "be continually filled" with the Spirit.

When we are continually filled and refilled, God's presence overflows our lives! As we spend time daily praying in the Spirit and asking God to fill us spiritually, we are actually recharging our "spiritual batteries" and receiving a fresh infilling of His power, presence, and love! It is there, in His presence, where we can hear His voice and receive directions for a new day.

Endnote

1. Kenneth E. Hagin, *He Gave Gifts to Men* (Tulsa: Kenneth Hagin Ministries, 1992), 22.

Chapter Eight

Caller I.D.

The heavens declare the glory of God; the skies proclaim the work of His hands (Psalm 19:1).

One gorgeous June evening in 1983, three of my sisters were enjoying the weather in the backyard of our parents' home in Gaithersburg, Maryland. Linda was listening to Christian music by Twila Paris, Karin was reading her Bible, and Krista was studying. Karin happened to look up into the sky as a strange gray cloud began to form. Curious, she called to her sisters and pointed to the heavens. The three stood there in awe and unbelief as they saw the form of Jesus with His arms outstretched. Tears streamed down their faces as the vision continued. Letters slowly began to form until the words "JESUS LOVES YOU" appeared! They slowly dissolved and were replaced by the words "JOY" and "SEE!" The entire vision lasted about 15 minutes. My sisters were stunned and overwhelmed that God would reveal Himself to them in this wonderful way!

My sisters *did see joy* that afternoon and danced around and worshiped God together!

* * *

The year before we married, my wife Crissy had a similar vision. While visiting her parents in Florida in 1982, she had gone outside at midnight on Christmas Eve after hearing church bells beckoning to her. Finding a small pond, she walked along its sandy beach, her gaze wandering about the starry heavens. To her amazement, she saw the perfect form of Jesus from the waist up with His arms outstretched to her! Unable to stand, she knelt down in the sand and wept with joy as she saw the Lord! She began to sing and dance before Him with wonder and awe that God would reveal Himself to her in such a special way!

Ever since hearing of these two incidents, every once in a while I too look up in the sky hoping to see something special!

Many Christians are waiting for a similar "burning bush" event in their lives or for God to speak to them audibly. Most often, however, God speaks to us through impressions in our spirits, or with what the Bible calls a "gentle whisper." Moses was 80 years old when the Lord appeared to him in a burning bush. Not many of us are willing to wait and pray 40 years in the wilderness for such an experience. Don't despair. Keep on believing. As we draw nearer and nearer to the endtimes, we will see more and more of these kind of dramatic experiences. God is raising up a new generation of prophets and apostles who will hear and see God in dramatic ways. Many people today are experiencing a greater awareness of God's presence, love, and a special intimacy with Him. Through the growing renewal that began in Toronto, and which has spread throughout the world, people are now experiencing God personally for the first time in their lives.

My eight-year-old daughter Valerie wants to experience God. I think we all do. Almost every night when she goes to bed she says to me, "Daddy, I want to see an angel." She then prays, "Jesus, I want to see You. I want to see an angel." I tell her to keep on believing and praying!

You may be thinking as you read this, "That's fine for you, but I've never heard God speak to me. How can I really know what God's voice sounds like? How can I know that He's really speaking to me?" I'd like to share with you four ways I've found that God speaks regularly to me and other people today. This is not an exclusive list, but it is a helpful place to begin.

Four Ways to Discern God's Voice

1. The Gentle Whisper

First Kings chapter 19 records Elijah's experience in meeting with God:

> *The Lord said, "Go out and stand on the mountain in the presence of the Lord, for the Lord is about to pass by." Then a great and powerful wind tore the mountains apart and shattered the rocks before the Lord,* **but the Lord was not in the wind**. *After the wind there was an earthquake,* **but the Lord was not in the earthquake**. *After the earthquake came a fire,* **but the Lord was not in the fire**. *And after the fire came* **a gentle whisper**. *When Elijah heard it, he pulled his cloak over his face and went out and stood at the mouth of the cave...* (1 Kings 19:11-13).

The gentle whisper—the quiet voice of God—is always speaking. Are you listening? God speaks to me in this fashion most often. I still have never heard an audible voice, although I know people who have. When I quiet myself before the Lord and wait, He speaks into my mind, my thoughts, or my heart. The key here is practice. The more that we wait and listen, the more we are able to recognize His voice in our spirits. When my wife calls me on the telephone and says, "Hello, Erik." I don't say, "Who is this?" No, I recognize her voice! As our good shepherd Jesus told us,

> *My sheep listen to My voice; I know them, and they follow Me* (John 10:27).

My friend Ilie was a shepherd boy in Romania. His brother, who owned a flock of sheep, sold them one day to a man in another village far away. One day, many years later, he visited the man who had bought the sheep. Seeing the sheep from a distance, he called out their names. Despite the passage of time, the sheep recognized his voice and came running to him!

Jesus calls us by name, and we should recognize His voice. It was with this gentle whisper that God called me to become a police officer. During a quiet time one day, I was praying about my future. Single at the time and attending the University of Maryland, I was the only born-again believer in my family of seven. In this quiet time, the Lord spoke into my mind with a "gentle whisper" three very specific things:

1. I would become a police officer in a particular department;
2. I would marry soon; and
3. My family would be saved soon.

I wrote these things down in my journal and prayed for them to come to pass.

* * *

I walked into the Executive Office Building in Rockville, Maryland, dressed in a beige polyester three-piece suit, complete with bell-bottom pants. Polyester was in style in those days, and besides, it was the only suit I had. I stepped into the elevator and rode up to the seventh floor. All the while, I was thinking, *This shouldn't be too hard. After all, God has led me to do this. Besides, there can't be that many people who want to be cops anyway.*

After spending an hour and a half filling out the forms, I turned them in to the lady at the personnel desk. My hand was sore from writer's cramp.

"What's the next step?" I asked.

"We'll contact you when we have approval for another academy class," she answered, "at which time you will be notified to take a written test."

"A test?" I said, a little surprised. *But I thought I'd get the job today. I mean, with my security experience and education in criminology....* The clerk cleared her throat, and I came out of my momentary fog.

"Is there anything else I can do for you?"

"Yes. How many people have applied so far?" (I thought my chances would be pretty good if there were only 50 or so.)

"We have around 500 applicants at this time."

My jaw dropped open: *500!*

"There must be a pretty big academy class then," I said, hopefully.

"Usually there are about 35-40 in a class. Oh, and I might add that at least half the class will be minority and/or female."

Thanking her, I left the building feeling very discouraged. The odds were against me!

I worked hard, though, and made it through the difficult written and oral board tests. Many candidates were being weeded out. Next came the background investigation and reference checks, then the grueling physical strength, stamina, and stress tests. I passed all these, and I was becoming more and more confident of my selection. Then came the medical exam.

Never having had any physical problems, I honestly thought that this would be a breeze. I wasn't prepared for the "windstorm," however, that was coming to test my faith. It began with a phone call one morning at my security office in a department store.

"Mr. Tammaru?" asked a woman.

"Yes, this is Erik Tammaru."

"I'm with the medical department of the county police, calling about the test results of your medical exam. Everything looks good except that your back X-ray shows some kind of irregularity. We would like you to have it checked out by a specialist tomorrow."

She then gave me the name and address of a doctor. Anxiety latched onto me like the handcuffs we used when arresting shoplifters. *There's nothing wrong with my back! That's crazy! I've never had any back problems, but what if….*

I went to the doctor's office that same week and checked in. After the usual wait, my doctor walked into the room carrying some X-rays.

"Mr. Tammaru?" he smiled.

"Yes," I replied nervously.

"I've got your X-rays here, but I don't know why they wanted you to come in." I breathed a sigh of relief. He wrinkled his brow and continued, "I don't even need to look at you. I can see very clearly that you have a congenital back problem."

Congenital back problem? There goes the job!

He tried explaining to me what the problem was, but I didn't really care or want to understand at that point. I was fighting discouragement.

"But, doctor," I said in desperation, "I've never had any trouble with my back. I'm totally healthy, and I've played sports all my life!"

"Well, bend over and let me take a look," he said as a concession. I leaned over and he ran his fingers up and down my backbone. "You appear to be okay, but the X-ray clearly shows this problem. I'm going to have to send them my report, which confirms the prognosis."

"What does that mean? Is the police department going to hire me or not?"

With a frown on his face he shook his head. "It's very doubtful. Unfortunately, you are at high risk for early disability. I'm sorry."

What's going on, God? You told me that I was going to be a policeman, and now this? All the way home in my car I kept asking the Lord, "Why, God? Why is this happening to me?" I decided to go for a walk and pray. I poured my heart out to Him and came to a little park where I laid down on a bench, feeling totally and utterly defeated. In a very clear and discernible voice, I heard God speak again to my spirit. It was the same voice that I had heard months before when God had first told me to become a policeman.

"Don't you believe in Me?" He said. "I told you that you would get the job, didn't I? It wasn't your idea, it was Mine! Trust in Me. Have faith in Me. *I will open every door that needs to be opened*, and you will get this job. Only believe!"

At that moment a peace came over me that I can't describe. Somehow I knew that God was going to perform what He had spoken. I was going to get this job. I only needed to wait and trust.

Weeks went by. The time for the new academy class was quickly approaching, and still I had heard nothing. These grueling weeks were testing my ability to trust God. He had spoken. Could I persevere in faith and hope? Finally, a week before the academy was to begin, I received notification that I was approved for the job! Apparently the back specialist had gone on vacation for two weeks and failed to mail in my report. After his return, he sent the report in to the medical department, but the doctor handling my case *just happened to be out sick*. Because of the rush, another stand-by doctor quickly certified my report! God had intervened and opened the door as He had promised!

* * *

Within the next 18 months, I had become a police officer, married my beautiful wife Crissy, and seen five out of six of my family members born again and water baptized! God was faithful in performing His word, just as He had promised. God will speak to you in the same way if you will take the time and allow Him to. Take time today to listen for that gentle whisper!

2. A Word Burning in Your Heart

Often the Lord confirms to me that He is speaking by causing the word to literally burn in my heart. The psalmist David knew of this experience:

My heart grew hot within me, and as I meditated, the fire burned; then I spoke with my tongue... (Psalm 39:3).

The first time I remember this happening to me was when the Lord spoke to me about marrying my wife Crissy. One morning as I was sitting behind the police station in my cruiser, the Lord suddenly said to me, "You are going to marry Crissy Doing." That was news to me, because up until that time we had only been friends at church. I didn't really know her well. Suddenly, my heart began to grow warm within me! As I meditated on what God had said, my heart grew hotter and hotter, and I knew within that Crissy was to be my bride. Unknown to me at the time, *two weeks earlier* the Lord had spoken to Crissy about me!

This phenomenon often occurs to me when I am supposed to give a public prophecy or word of knowledge in church. As the Lord gives me a Scripture or word to share, my heart sometimes becomes hot, or I feel a pressure there. When that happens, I know that I am to share it publicly. Maybe that's already happened to you, but you didn't know what it was. Be sensitive to the Spirit—perhaps He'll speak to you in this way as well.

3. Visions and Dreams

We are told in the Book of Acts and the Book of Joel that in the last days God would pour out His Spirit on all people and that He would speak to us through visions and dreams (see Acts 2:17; Joel 2:28).

As we seek God in our prayer times, we need to be open both to visions that we can see in our minds as well as open visions and trances (the kind that Peter experienced in Acts chapter 10). Often, God will give a picture in the mind with some kind of interpretation.

For example, one Sunday as we were praying for a woman visitor in our church in Switzerland, a member of our church saw a vision in his mind. His eyes were closed, and he saw that the woman had a problem in her uterus and that she was having trouble conceiving. This church member hadn't known anything about the woman. However, she and her husband began to cry as they realized that God saw and cared about their needs. Shortly after this, the husband converted to Christ and threw away all his drugs!

I have already shared how the Lord called us to Europe through a vision of a field full of tulips and of various European flags, which resulted later that year in a mission trip with a team of 17 people to Romania, Austria, and Holland! God will speak to us in visions and dreams if we seek Him.

4. A Thought or Word Out of Place

I shared in Chapter Four how the Lord spoke to me about a divine appointment while I was standing in line to buy pizza. At that moment, a divine appointment was probably the furthest thing from my mind. It was totally out of place and context for the situation that I was in. I was meditating on a mouth-watering piece of pepperoni pizza, not on how I could lead someone to Christ! Nevertheless, the Lord was preparing me for a witnessing opportunity with Eddie Murray, the professional baseball player.

If a thought comes into your mind and gets your attention because it seems strange or out of place, get ready! The Lord may be speaking to you.

Another example of this is when I was pursuing the drunk driver I spoke of in Chapter Seven. I was concentrating on catching my man, not on praying or seeking God. Yet the words came into my mind so clearly, "Don't you trust Me? Don't give up yet!" I knew that it was God because of the context of the situation.

Sometimes it happens that someone stands out to me in a crowd. I can be on a busy street, in a shopping mall, or even at a large concert, and find myself drawn to one particular person.

I attended "Jesus '86" in Pennsylvania, where over 20,000 people gathered to hear good preaching, listen to Christian music, and enjoy camping in the countryside. One evening while Josh McDowell was speaking, I was wandering around the huge campgrounds and praying. As I drew near to the main stage area, I noticed a woman dressed in white. As I walked past her, I couldn't shake the impression that I was supposed to talk with her. I didn't know why, but she stood out to me. There were thousands of other people around, yet I felt drawn to her. Not knowing what to do, I went back to my tent and shared my impressions with my wife. Crissy encouraged me to go back and see if the woman was still there, because it seemed obvious to her that the Lord wanted me to speak with this lady.

Gathering up my courage, I made my way back to the main stage area and, sure enough, there she was! Taking a deep breath, I finally introduced myself to her.

"Excuse me," I said nervously, "My name's Erik. This might seem strange, but I feel that the Lord has shown me that I'm supposed to talk to you."

Immediately the woman began to cry. As she wiped the tears away, the Lord gave me words of encouragement for her.

She looked up at me, smiled a half smile, and said, "You don't know who I am, do you?"

Thinking I should recognize her, I searched my brain. *Is she a famous preacher? A singer? Should I know her?* I didn't have a clue.

"No," I said as she composed herself. "I'm sorry. Should I know you?"

She laughed and blew her nose into a tissue.

"I'm the wife of ——. He's about to do his concert after the current speaker finishes. You don't realize the encouragement that you have brought to my heart tonight. You see, we've been on such a stressful concert tour and…" her voice began to break up again. "Well, I needed the encouragement. Thanks."

She was the wife of one of the most popular Christian musicians there at the time, one who had an international audience. The Lord had wanted me to bring a word of comfort and encouragement to one of His precious children during a very stressful time in her life.

All of us have the opportunity to hear from God in a very special way! The King of kings is waiting for a time to meet with you today—to share His heart with you. Take some time *now* to listen to His voice. Maybe He'll speak with a gentle whisper, or maybe your heart will grow hot, or maybe you'll see visions or have prophetic dreams. Take the time to listen. The more you listen, the more you will learn to discern the voice of the Lord. Open your heart and mind to Him and ask Him to speak to you and help you learn to recognize His voice. I guarantee that you will not be disappointed!

Chapter Nine

Oikos: Winning Family and Friends to Christ

"The Lord will do everything by prayer, and nothing without prayer."

—John Wesley

"What is the link between being touched by God and walking in the Spirit? Prayer!"

—Frank Damazio[1]

I was the first "born-again" believer among my family and circle of friends. After my conversion, I felt a special burden to pray for and reach out to these important people in my life. You probably feel the same way about those closest to you who do not know the Lord. Take heart, for there is hope! Salvation is a central theme throughout the Scriptures, especially in the New Testament. In the Book of Acts, Dr. Luke describes how *entire families* and *households* were saved, many simultaneously. For example, Acts chapter 16 tells how Lydia and her household were saved and baptized *together*. Later in the same chapter Luke records the conversion of the Philippian jailer and his entire family, and their baptism by Paul and Silas. There are other similar stories throughout the Scriptures.

"*Oikos*" Evangelism

The Greek word *oikos* is the word most commonly used in the New Testament to refer to one's house or household. For example, in Acts chapter 16, the Philippian jailer and his *household* (*oikos*) were saved and baptized. The meaning of *oikos* extends beyond simply "family" or "household," however, to include one's sphere of influence: those 10-20 people whom one cares for, has regular contact with, and has influence over. Today, each of us has an *oikos* of family and friends—people we see on a regular basis.

Each of us is called to reach our individual "*oikos*" for Jesus Christ! That is our mission field. If you are the first "born-again" believer in your family, be encouraged! God has specifically chosen you and given you a place of influence and leadership to reach your friends and loved ones for Him!

It was said of Jesus that He was a friend of tax collectors and sinners, a drinker and a glutton. In other words, He was where the heathen were. In His own words, "It is not the healthy who need a doctor, but the sick" (Mt. 9:12). He went to where the people were.

Oikos evangelism involves relating to our families and friends. *This means that we must spend time with them.* After their conversions, many Christians begin to draw back from their "sinful, unbelieving" friends. Afraid of being polluted by the world, these babes in Christ effectively remove themselves from their greatest spheres of influence. The best thing you can do to help to lead the people in your *oikos* to Christ is to be with them. Let them see the new you! Let them experience the love of God flowing through you!

The opposite is also true. The very worst thing you can do to your chances of reaching those around you is to cut yourself off from them. How are you going to fish where there are no fish? Can you imagine a fisherman getting up early, driving an hour, then hiking another hour into the woods only to cast his line into a lake that had no fish? There might even be a sign there that says, "No fish here." Crazy? Maybe, but Christians do it all the time.

We hold crusades and evangelistic outreaches in our churches that are attended only by saved people. There are no fish to be seen for miles! Why? I believe the reason that there are so few lost people attending our churches and meetings is that we feel uncomfortable spending time with unbelievers anymore. Our only fellowship is at Denny's after the meeting—with other Christians. Are we afraid of unbelievers? Are we afraid that our "holy ears" will be offended by some foul language? (*Some believers, though, have no problem fellowshiping for hours on end with a foul-mouthed, uncouth, ill-mannered, violent, immoral, and sex-crazed companion—their TV set! Can you figure it?*)

This doesn't mean that we should enter into the sinful lifestyles of our unsaved friends. On the contrary, we can show them that life can be fun and enjoyable without the vices of sin. Jesus commanded us to be salt and light for the world. How can we be light if we hide under a bushel? Salt, likewise, serves no useful purpose just sitting in the shaker. If we don't start "seasoning" the world with the flavor of Christ, be assured that He will start shaking the "salt shaker," that is, the Church, until we get a move on. In Acts chapter 8, a great persecution broke out against the Church, resulting in the scattering of the believers throughout the world of their day. They had been slow to obey the Lord's command to "go into all the world." This persecution provided the stimulus for the Church to do what Christ intended from the beginning. *One way or another, they were going!*

Reaching Your Family

One morning as I was praying for my family, the Holy Spirit said to me,

"Invite your sister Linda to church this Sunday. Read the parable of the sower during the worship time, and she will be saved."

At this, my heart began to grow hot within me, as I described in the last chapter. That was how I knew that God was speaking to me and that I had to obey Him! So I called Linda, I invited her to church, and she accepted. That Sunday morning I went forward during the worship time with my Bible in my hands and my knees shaking. Before the entire church I read the parable of the sower (see Mt. 13:3-9,18-23) and gave this short interpretation:

"The seed sown among the thorns represents people here today who have heard the Word of God, but the cares of this life (money, friends, career, etc.) are choking that seed from bearing fruit in your life. Is there anyone here today, and this is speaking to you? God is calling you to be like that seed that will produce a hundredfold fruit. If that is you, please raise your hand so that we can pray with you."

My sister told me later that as she sat there she knew immediately that the word was for her. Her heart racing, she struggled inwardly and resisted. At that point, she told me, something literally grabbed her arm and pulled it into the air! She came forward and prayed with our pastor to receive Christ! That same afternoon we baptized her at a church member's house. God was true to His word!

One by one, every member of my immediate family has come to Christ. I am convinced that prayer played a crucial role. Just as Leroy's family had been faithful in prayer for him, we should be faithful in praying for our unsaved family members as well as look actively for ways to reach our individual *oikos* for Jesus.

When I prayed for my family, I took Jesus' promise literally:

> *I will give you the keys of the kingdom of heaven; what-*
> *ever you bind on earth will be bound in heaven, and*
> *whatever you loose on earth, will be loosed in heaven*
> (Matthew 16:19).

Before they became Christians, three of my sisters were in relationships with unsaved young men. I prayed for them according to Matthew 16:19:

> "Father, You have given me the keys of the Kingdom.
> Whatever I loose on earth will be loosed in Heaven.
> Father, in Jesus' name I loose my sisters from these
> ungodly relationships, and I ask You to lead them to
> You. Amen!"

We even prayed for them in our weekly Friday morning prayer group. In a short time, Lisa's boyfriend broke up with her. She came to Christ soon after. Then Linda's boyfriend broke up with her and, finally, so did Karin's! We have been given power and authority to really see our loved ones saved. Begin praying according to Matthew 16:19, and take authority in the Spirit to claim your loved ones for God.

Reaching Your Friends

Oikos evangelism works for friends as well! My three closest friends—Jeff, Frank, and Mike— all came to know Christ as Lord within a two-year time frame. Once again, I believe prayer was the integral key to their conversions. I spent hours praying for my family and my friends to come to a saving knowledge of Jesus Christ. It was during those prayer times that the Lord gave me instructions and wisdom as to how I was to be involved in the process. I was not to be simply a bystander and watch God work, but I was an active participant in every one of these precious conversions! Of the nine people mentioned (six family members and three friends), I had the privilege of sharing my faith and testimony in detail with them all. I was also privileged to be able to to personally baptize seven of them! You are no different. You should be actively praying for *and* reaching out to your lost friends. God *wants* us to reach our "*oikos*"! You *have an anointing* to pray for and to share with your precious family members and friends.

My friend Frank had an especially powerful conversion experience. He and I had known each other since grade school, and for over ten years, he had been one of my closest buddies. After my conversion, I tried on several occasions to share with Frank, but I had always ran up against a brick wall.

"Oh no!" he would laugh at me. "You're one of those 'reborns'!"

I continued to pray for him regularly, especially that the Lord would bring other Christians into his life. I was living together with six other single men from my church at the time, and we decided to hold an evangelistic party one Friday evening at our household. We sent out invitations, prepared food and drinks, and set up a multimedia slide presentation telling about the life of our church. It was a great evening as about 15 of our unbelieving friends showed up, including Frank and his two sisters. We ate and talked for a while, then showed the multimedia presentation, hoping to open people's hearts to talk about spiritual things.

I asked Frank what he thought about the slide show.

"I'm impressed," Frank smiled. "That was a quality production, and your church seems very interesting. I especially liked the part that showed how all of you really seem to live out your faith. It really is real to you, isn't it?"

Frank was very open, and we talked for half an hour. I then suggested that we go into the other room to pray, along with his sister Diana and my wife Crissy (who was still only a friend at that time). As we began to pray, the Holy Spirit suddenly came upon Frank with incredible supernatural conviction! He began to weep uncontrollably and to shake. Then he shouted with a loud voice, "Oh God, help me! Oh God, forgive me!" It was similar to one of the experiences I had read about that had happened in meetings with Charles Finney or Jonathan Edwards, *but this was happening to my friend*! It created such a commotion that many of the people in the other room came running to see what was happening! Frank's youngest sister Margie was in the other room when it happened, and she was overwhelmed by the whole situation. Frank continued to weep as we began to pray over him. Then, as suddenly as it had begun, the conviction stopped. Frank's face shone like an angel, as he somehow knew in his spirit that he was cleansed and forgiven. He lifted up his face, smiled, and said, "I'm saved!" He looked so at peace in his heart at that moment. I'll never forget it.

That night, full of rejoicing, we filled the bathtub and water-baptized Frank, his sister Diana, and his sister Margie, who had received Christ shortly after Frank. God is in the business of saving households and families! It was Acts chapter 16, and it was happening in 1983.

Oikos Evangelism in Action

Jeff and I have been good buddies since junior high school when we played baseball and soccer and generally just "hung out" together. A humorous incident that happened during a baseball game when we were both 16 should provide an idea of what our relationship was like.

It was a midsummer night, 90+ degrees and humid—a typical summer night in the Washington, D.C., area—and our team, the South Bowie Boys Club, was in the middle of an important game. I was pitching that evening, and Jeff was catching. A relatively large crowd of parents, siblings, and friends had assembled to watch our game. In the bottom of the last inning we held a two-run lead when the opposing team came to bat. We were only three outs away from victory. Jeff signaled me for a "knuckle ball." I wound up and threw. In the humid, windless night air the ball didn't dance, but just floated in nice and fat. The batter slapped a line-drive single to centerfield. Bummer!

The next batter came up. I struggled and, after five pitches, walked him. Now, with runners on first and second, the winning run came to the plate.

"Time out!" Jeff yelled, whipping off his mask as he ran out to the mound to meet me. I was fully expecting encouraging words of wisdom like, "Come on, Erik. We can get these guys out," etc. etc. Instead, Jeff grinned from ear to ear and said, "So, what are you doing after the game tonight?"

Surprised by the unexpected question, I could only stammer, but with a grin of my own. "I don't know. What do you want to do?"

"I'll invite the girls, and you get the beer," he joked.

I burst out laughing, and Jeff trotted back to home plate. With the pressure now off, I calmed down and was able to retire the side, and we won the game without any further problems. I don't remember now if we went out after the game, but that's the kind of camaraderie Jeff and I enjoyed as friends.

After I became a Christian, I didn't want to lose my friendship with Jeff, but I also knew that our relationship couldn't continue as it was before. What was I to do? Honestly afraid to tell him that I had become a Christian, I decided simply to continue to be a friend. We got together at least once a week for the next six months. Sometimes we met on the golf course, sometimes at home for dinner and ping-pong, and sometimes, even, in a local bar. Throughout this time our friendship remained intact, and I had many opportunities to share my new faith naturally. I was able to remain pure in my walk with Christ without being "religious." I didn't ram the gospel down his throat or hit him over the head with my Bible, but I tried to be natural and normal around him so that he could see the change in me. After a few months, I even invited him to a cell group meeting. As we all worshiped, Jeff sat there with his head lowered, staring at the floor. I thought to myself, *Oh no, this is too much for him. I've scared him away.* To my surprise, however, he was very open to the gospel.

The breakthrough occurred after I had spent considerable time in prayer for him. The Lord spoke into my heart to buy Jeff the car stereo power booster he had been wanting. A month later, Jeff became a believer and joined our fellowship. I believe that the gesture of my gift showed him that I really cared.

It was similar with my friend Mike. Close friends since childhood, when our mothers would literally bathe us together, I called him "Gikol" and he called me "Rick." We spent many vacations together through the years, since he lived in Pittsburgh and my family lived five hours away in Maryland. During our teen years, we spent a lot of time at the beach, even making a couple of trips to Daytona Beach, Florida, during spring break. At that time, we were not the most well-behaved boys, either. Again, after I became a Christian, I had a strong burden for my friend. What should I do?

The summer after my conversion, Mike called about our annual Ocean City, Maryland, trip. Normally, we would drive to the beach in either of our "muscle cars" (I had a Pontiac LeMans convertible with a 400-cubic-inch motor, and he owned a souped-up Plymouth GTX with a 440-cubic-inch motor), then camp out at a nearby campground. Our favorite activity was eating massive quantities of steamed Maryland crabs, seasoned with Old Bay. We enjoyed the beach, of course, and then carousing at night. Was I to tell him that I was now a Christian and couldn't do the things that we used to do? Should I just cancel?

I felt that I needed to be honest with him, tell him about the change in my life, and go with him again. We had a great time together in Ocean City that year. I had a chance to really share my heart with him and live out my faith. Instead of bar-hopping, for example, I went for walks on the beach at night. Mike didn't get saved that year, but the following summer he did! I had the joyful privilege of baptizing him that next year. I was able to be a part of his conversion because I remained his friend and spent valuable time with him.

Oikos **Evangelism on the Mission Field**

My wife and I have tried to use these same principles on the mission field as well. When we first arrived in Austria in 1992, we could barely speak German. Fortunately for us, many of our neighbors spoke some English. While I was away with a team in Romania, Crissy began to meet our neighbors. She was often invited for coffee and cake (called *jause*—pronounced "yow-sah") in the afternoon and began developing friendships. It was (and usually is) slow going. We also made many a "faux pas" (figurative foot in the mouth) as we were learning a new language. For example, one time Crissy wanted to ask our neighbor Claudia if she made her cake with confectioner's sugar (*staubzucker*), and was puzzled when Claudia began laughing hysterically. Crissy had gotten mixed up and asked if Claudia had made her cake with a vacuum cleaner (*staubsauger*)!

Perseverance pays off, though, because after about a year, one of Crissy's coffee friends, Evelyn, prayed to receive Christ. A few months later, another woman, Irene, prayed with Crissy and was reunited with her husband. We have met dozens of other precious people in this way, and each of them is nearer to knowing the Lord. *The key is spending time!*

I met Alfred, an Austrian friend, at the United Nations in Vienna. We used to go to the sauna together twice a month. Over the past three years we have developed a very good friendship. Just as I was becoming discouraged about the slow progress with him, Alfred surprised me by inviting me to a Thanksgiving dinner that a friend of his had invited him to attend. I was happy to go with Alfred. I received another surprise when I learned that the dinner was held in a Baptist church with an American pastor! In addition, Alfred's other friend just happened to also be a Christian. Sometimes the fruit is a long time in coming, but with faith and patience we will inherit the promises of God (see Heb. 6:12)!

Are you willing to spend time reaching out to your family and friends? What would Jesus do? Where would He be?

God wants to save your *oikos* as well. He wants to use you as a prayer instrument to bring your family, your friends, your work colleagues, your neighbors, your carpool members, your bank teller, your barber, the man at the bus stop, the widow across the street, the parents of your kid's school friends, etc., into a personal relationship with Jesus! It's our *job* and *privilege* to pray for and look for opportunities to reach our *oikos* for Jesus!

Consistent in Prayer

If you were to look back on your life, you would certainly find that someone was consistently praying for your salvation. Leroy's mother and sister were praying consistently for him. They saw the fruit of their prayers. I know that my great-grandmother Peters prayed for me from the day that she knew I was in my mother's womb. My mother had German measles when she was pregnant with me, so many family members had prayed for my health before I was born. On the day of my birth, my great-grandmother took me in her arms and exclaimed, "This little love baby must have a special call of God on his life. The Lord has protected him in the womb." My grandmother Hughes bathes me in prayer even to this day, and my mother also actively prayed for me during my more rebellious teenage years. I am certain that my salvation can be attributed to the faithful and consistent prayers of loved ones.

My friend Ché Ahn, pastor of Harvest Rock Church in Pasadena, California, had an interesting conversion. One day during his rebellious teen years, he was driving with a friend in his neighborhood. A Christian family took note of him and decided to make him a regular on their prayer list. Shortly thereafter, Ché had a dramatic confrontation with the Lord while at a Deep Purple rock concert at the Baltimore Civic Center. During a break in the concert, he was enjoying a drug-induced high and began to think to himself, *So, this is what it means to feel close to God.* Suddenly two young men walked up to him, pointed at him, and said, "You think you are close to God, but you are not. You need to get your life in order and surrender to Jesus Christ as Lord." They then turned and walked away. Ché was so shaken by this that he immediately left the concert! He surrendered his life to Jesus and has served Him ever since. It all began, however, with faithful and consistent prayers from someone who cared.

Prayer List

What are the practical implications of all of this? I recommend that you sit down and make out a prayer list. Include on it the names of those in your family and all those in your *oikos* sphere of influence We all have many prayer requests and intercession needs, but I think that we can all carve out at least one day a week to focus our prayers on our *oikos* list.

For example, here is a sample weekly intercession list:

- Sunday—Pray for your church and its leaders.
- Monday—Pray for your city and your nation, including their governments and respective leaders.
- Tuesday—Pray for the people on your *oikos* list by name.
- Wednesday—Pray for people in your home group and/or church.
- Thursday—Pray for revival to come to your city and nation.
- Friday—Pray for special needs—an evangelistic outreach, a need in the local church, etc.
- Saturday—Pray for protection, blessing, and health for your children and family.

Obviously you can change or adapt this list to your own situation. Note also that this is in addition to your regular time of worship, thanksgiving, verse memorization, and personal prayer petitions. I have found it helpful to have an established intercession agenda. Intercession is hard work! Just like everything else, if we don't plan our intercession, we won't accomplish much!

If you make the effort to pray regularly for the people on your *oikos* list, the Lord will give you specific wisdom and guidance on how *best* to reach these people for Jesus. Many times as I prayed for my family or friends, the Lord showed me creative ways to bless them or reach out to them, such as the Christmas that the Lord told me to buy something *out of the ordinary* for my friend Jeff. Normally, we had exchanged small gifts for one another, but one year the Lord said, "Buy him that car stereo component that he's been wanting." And, as I stated earlier, one month later, Jeff became a believer and joined our fellowship.

The key is being sensitive to the Spirit's voice as we pray for our friends. Remember, it's a two-way conversation. God will use *you* as a part of the process of reaching your family and friends, and *you* will see the fruit of your hard labors! The key is, stay consistent, don't give up, and keep on loving those folks on your *oikos* list! You won't be disappointed!

Endnote

1. Frank Damazio, *The Making of a Leader* (Portland: Bible Temple Publishing, 1990).

Part Four

Transforming Our World

But you will receive power when the Holy Spirit comes on you; and you will be My witnesses...to the ends of the earth (Acts 1:8).

"This is no age to advocate restraint; the church today does not need to be restrained, but to be aroused, to be awakened, to be filled with a spirit of glory, for she is failing in the modern world."

—D. Martyn Lloyd-Jones

Chapter Ten

Get Out of the Boat!

"Come," He said. Then Peter got down out of the boat, walked on the water and came toward Jesus (Matthew 14:29).

One Sunday morning I received a phone call from Isabelle, a member of Oikos International Church Fellowship in Basel, Switzerland.

"Sali Erik," she said in Swiss German, "I was wondering if you could help me?"

"Sure," I replied. "What can I do for you?"

"A woman near us whom we have been reaching out to has a very sick baby. The baby has been in the hospital for weeks with some kind of lung virus and infection. She has coughed so much and had such a difficult time breathing that the doctors have put her on oxygen."

"How old is the baby?"

"Five months," Isabelle continued. "Her mother Astrid is very worried. She wants us to dedicate the baby to the Lord or baptize her as an assurance that she will go to Heaven if she dies."

"I see," I said, thinking about the possible ramifications. "Where is she now?"

"She's home today for a few hours, but she goes back into the hospital tonight at 8:00 p.m. for more treatment and care. Could you please call Astrid and talk to her?"

Trying to prepare for my Sunday meeting, I was a little irritated by the interruption. I called Astrid later that morning and tried to convince her to bring the baby to church where I could pray for her. She said that she couldn't get out, so I made an appointment to visit her and her baby, whose name was Sandy, after our church service, which would end at 6:00 p.m.

I took along with me Rene, Isabelle's husband, to pray for baby Sandy. Rene had previously shared his faith with Astrid and knew where she lived.

Astrid's apartment was in a lower income area of Basel. Still dressed in my sport jacket and tie, I felt very out of place in this neighborhood, and even more so when Astrid opened the door. She and her husband, an Albanian Muslim, looked like throwbacks to the 1970's: long hair, T-shirts, and jeans. The numerous black-light posters on the walls also reminded me of the drug culture I had experienced as a teen in the 70's.

Making things even more awkward, Astrid's husband and teenage son sat in the living room watching a loud soccer match on TV. After explaining to Astrid what I was going to do, I anointed baby Sandy with oil according to James 5:14-15:

Is any one of you sick? He should call the elders of the church to pray over him and anoint him with oil in the name of the Lord. And the prayer offered in faith will make the sick person well (James 5:14-15a).

Sandy, who had been very quiet and peaceful the entire time we were there, began to cough violently the instant the oil touched her forehead. The Holy Spirit was touching her little body! We continued to pray, commanding the virus to leave in the name of Jesus. The coughing continued even harder until suddenly Sandy coughed out a large amount of greenish-gray mucous. Then she became quiet and peaceful once more, smiling up at us. We felt in our hearts that God had healed her!

Sandy went back into the hospital an hour later as scheduled, and was to be there indefinitely.

The next day I received a phone call. "Hello, Erik?" a voice said excitedly. "It's me, Astrid. I just wanted you to know that Sandy came home from the hospital today! The doctors ran an oxygen level test on her lungs and the levels are normal! I know that God healed her. *It really is a miracle!*"

The following Sunday, Astrid, her teenage son, and Sandy were in our church service, where Sandy was dedicated to the Lord!

Get Outside the Four Walls

As I shared earlier, it is time for the Church to arise and bring her message back to the streets and into the world where the sick and needy people are. For too long we have been satisfied to sit back and wait for unbelievers to come to us. We think, *If only my friend would come to church on Sunday, my pastor will get him saved.* Maybe that's because we have a false understanding that ministry is the pastor's job or the evangelist's job. *No!* Scripture makes it *very* clear that ministry is the job of the Church—*me and you.* The pastor's job is to *equip* and *train* the Church to do the works of ministry! Paul leaves no doubt of this in his letter to the Ephesians:

> *It was He who gave some to be apostles, some to be prophets, some to be evangelists, and some to be pastors and teachers,* **to prepare God's people for works of service**, *so that the body of Christ may be built up* (Ephesians 4:11-12).

We need to get outside the four walls of our churches and into our communities with the *message* and the *power* of the gospel!

I must confess, as a pastor, that I often do the same thing. When Astrid first called me that Sunday, I tried to coax her into coming to our church service that day. There is a comfort and security in praying for someone in a church service with the praise team playing and all the church members there supporting you. It takes guts to go into the real world and confront the darkness on the devil's turf. Think about this, though: It also takes a lot of courage for an unbeliever to come into one of our church services! We can be an imposing group of people. It was too big of a step for Astrid to come to our meeting, but she was very open to me visiting her and praying for her sick child. After Sandy was healed, she was then ready for the culture shock of our Sunday meeting.

Allow me to ask a few questions. Did Jesus minister more in synagogues, or among the people? When Jesus was casting out demons, did He have the worship band play a couple of rousing "fight songs" to get the mood just right? When He prayed for the sick, did He invite them to church first? Or did He go to them? *Jesus was among the people.* Yes, He also ministered in the synagogues and in the temple, but most of His amazing miracles occurred outside of those four walls!

It's time for us to get outside of our comfort zones—out of the boat—and into the place of faith and ministry, which often is out on the water with Jesus. He's calling us there—He's calling *you* there—to meet Him in the supernatural place!

On the Water

I love the story of Peter walking on the water, because it shows what the Lord desires for us regarding the supernatural realm:

> *Immediately Jesus made the disciples get into the boat and go on ahead of Him to the other side, while He dismissed the crowd. After He had dismissed them, He went up on a mountainside by Himself to pray. When evening came, He was there alone, but the boat was*

already a considerable distance from land, buffeted by the waves because the wind was against it. During the fourth watch of the night Jesus went out to them, walking on the lake. When the disciples saw Him walking on the lake, they were terrified. "It's a ghost," they said, and cried out in fear. But Jesus immediately said to them: "Take courage! It is I. Don't be afraid." "Lord, if it's You," Peter replied, "tell me to come to You on the water." "Come," He said. Then Peter got down out of the boat, walked on the water and came toward Jesus. But when he saw the wind, he was afraid and, beginning to sink, cried out, "Lord, save me!" Immediately Jesus reached out His hand and caught him. "You of little faith," He said, "why did you doubt?" And when they climbed into the boat, the wind died down. Then those who were in the boat worshiped Him, saying, "Truly You are the Son of God" (Matthew 14:22-33).

When the disciples first saw Jesus on the water, they were terrified. The same is true of us today. When the Lord begins to reveal His power among us, like the disciples, many of us are terrified. We cry out, "Lord, is that really You? That doesn't fit my picture of who You are." Recent outpourings of God's Spirit in renewal around the world have unnerved many Christians. Calling these outpourings "emotionalism" or outright "unbiblical," many are missing out on the opportunity to "walk on the water" and meet the Lord. Yes, we should carefully "test everything," and "hold on to the good" (see 1 Thess. 5:21). Yet many believers don't even do that. Instead, they simply try to avoid anything that scares them, or run away from anything they don't understand. Peter didn't let fear hold him back from personally experiencing the unknown realm of the supernatural.

Peter's response is necessary to a supernatural ministry:

"Lord, I don't understand all of this, but it sure appears to be You out there on the water. If it really is You, Lord, then call me to come to You."

He was willing to check it out and experience it firsthand, even at the risk of getting wet! When the Lord tells us to do something that may seem a little strange, we should respond with this same attitude, "Lord, if it's You, tell me to come, and I'll come."

When the Lord told me to take off Dennis' handcuffs and pray for him in my police car, it struck me as a little odd. But I was confident that He was there on the water calling me, so I "jumped out of the boat."

Jesus' response to Peter after he asked for permission to walk on the water excites me! He didn't say, "No, Peter, stay in the boat. Supernatural ministry is reserved for the Godhead only," or "No, Peter! You are not spiritually mature enough for such an important ministry," or "I'm sorry, water miracles, such as the parting of the Red Sea, passed away with the Old Testament dispensation." No! He clearly said, and I can imagine a smile on His face as He said it, "Come on, Peter! You can do it!"

That is His call to each and every one of us. Jesus also said, "I tell you the truth, anyone who has faith in Me will do what I have been doing. He will do even *greater* things than these, because I am going to the Father" (Jn. 14:12). Isn't that great news?

Natural and Supernatural

Peter's next action was amazing. He took a step of faith and stepped out of the boat! Was this first step natural or supernatural? It was a *natural* step. Anyone can step out of a boat. It was also a step of faith. If Jesus didn't meet him immediately, he was going to sink real fast. If we want to be used by God in the supernatural realm, then we must be willing to take that first, natural step of faith. Perhaps it's laying our hands on a sick person on the street for healing or sharing that impression or word of knowledge with your unbelieving friend. Maybe it's praying deliverance for that junkie or homeless person whom God directs you to pray for. The first step is your responsibility. The second, or supernatural, step is God's responsibility.

One evening, my wife and I attended a Christian fund-raising banquet with hundreds in attendance. As we were eating dinner, I noticed a teenage boy at the table adjacent to us. He was sitting with his parents and yet stood out to me for some reason. Then the Holy Spirit spoke into my heart, *This young man is involved in fornication. His girlfriend's name is Shelly.* I had just received what the Bible calls a "word of knowledge."

What am I to do with this? I felt that I should speak with him. Not wanting to embarrass him in front of his parents, I waited for him to get up from the table. When he finally did so, I hurried over to him. I simply introduced myself to him and took a natural step of faith.

"Do you have a girlfriend named Shelly?"

Shocked and a little confused he answered, "Yeah, that's right. Her name is Michelle, but I call her Shelly."

Knowing that the Lord had successfully met me on the water, I took the second and *supernatural* step. "The Lord spoke to me at the table during dinner. He told me that you're sleeping with Shelly and that as a Christian you need to stop."

His look of surprise and bewilderment told me that the Lord had hit the nail on the head. I spoke with him for a while, and then prayed with him. God wanted to restore a lost lamb in the flock!

I had taken the first natural step of sharing the impression with the young man. It was the same with baby Sandy. I obeyed God's Word to anoint her with oil. The healing process was up to God. We need to be willing to try, and, yes, perhaps to fail. I've had wrong impressions about people too! Fortunately, Jesus is always right there to help us.

As Peter took his eyes off of Jesus, and allowed the situation to bring fear into his heart, he began to sink. Jesus' response is the assurance we need if we are to take the risks of a supernatural ministry. He simply reached out His hand and pulled Peter out of the sea. So if we "get in a little over our heads," we can be assured that the Lord is always there to answer our cry for help! It's the Lord's will that we meet Him on the water! He wants to use every one of us in the supernatural realm. You have gifts from the Lord. If you are baptized in the Holy Spirit (as discussed earlier in Chapter Seven), you have spiritual gifts at your disposal to minister God's love to a dying world.

Jesus is moving powerfully in the earth today, and there is a wave of renewal and refreshing bringing healing and restoration to hundreds of thousands in the Body of Christ all over the world. Why? Is it to bless the Church and make us feel good? Is it to give us goosebumps? Is it to impress people with supernatural things? No! It is a preparation for the wave of revival and awakening that is coming soon! When we as Christians are healed and restored, we will carry out our commission to take it to the streets and bring healing and restoration to a lost world!

Chapter Eleven

Don't Forget the Gifts!

Follow the way of love and eagerly desire spiritual gifts... (1 Corinthians 14:1).

For this reason I remind you to fan into flame the gift of God, which is in you... (2 Timothy 1:6).

Annie and her husband, who were both heroin junkies with long criminal records, were under arrest for shoplifting in our police district. They had stolen food from a grocery store and were now sitting in the county jail awaiting their trial dates. Annie's veins had been so abused and damaged from shooting up that she had begun injecting the heroin into her fingers through filthy needles. While waiting in jail, she had developed gangrene in one of her hands and was rushed to the hospital for treatment with intravenous antibiotics. It was very difficult to find a vein that would support the IV. Still a prisoner, Annie was guarded by a police officer around the clock at the hospital. That's where I came in.

During one midnight shift, I received the hospital guard detail. Such duty was a welcome break from the routine of police patrol, and I also enjoyed such assignments because I knew that often a divine appointment awaited me. Tonight it was Annie. For almost four hours straight I was able to share my testimony and the gospel quite clearly with Annie. Although she was open, she was not yet ready to surrender her life to Jesus. I drove home early that morning with a heavy burden on my heart for her salvation. The following evening I had regular patrol duty, but before my shift was over my sergeant informed me that I would have guard duty again the next day.

I came home and told Crissy that I was going to have a second chance with Annie. As we were driving on the beltway to a home group meeting later that evening, we decided to pray for my time with Annie. As we prayed, Crissy received a vision from the Lord. She saw a wedding ring in her mind. The Lord then revealed to Crissy that Annie had lost her wedding ring and that this had troubled her greatly. He said that Annie was just like that lost ring, and because He loved her so much, He was seeking her. Crissy told me what she saw, and we prayed that I would have the opportunity to share it with Annie.

Later that night, around 11:00 p.m., I began my guard duty at the hospital. When I walked into the room, Annie greeted me with a smile.

"So you're on duty again tonight, huh?"

"Yeah, I guess you're stuck with me," I grinned, holding a brown paper sack behind my back. "Here," I said, extending the bag to her, "I brought you a couple of magazines and chocolate bars."

"Wow, thanks," she said, with a simultaneous look of surprise and embarrassment. "That's really nice of you." She turned her head away quickly as she tried to hold back the emotion that came as a result of one small act of kindness.

"I thought you might be a little bored lying around here all day," I said, trying to break up the tension. "It's just a little something to cheer you up. No big deal."

We chatted a while, and then taking a deep breath, I finally got up the courage to mention Crissy's vision.

"Annie," I said, looking straight at her, "this might sound like a strange question, but did you ever lose your wedding ring?"

"How did you know that?"

"God told my wife last night when we were praying for you."

"God told her?" she asked incredulously.

"Sure. Remember how I told you that we can have a personal relationship with God?"

"Well, yes…."

"That's what I'm talking about. Christianity is not a religion. It's not about going to some old church building to listen to organ music. It's about getting to know Jesus Christ as your Lord, your Savior, and your friend." I was excited at this point. "You know, the Lord also told my wife that you are just like that wedding ring."

"What do you mean?" she said, leaning forward.

"He said that you searched and searched for that ring, and it caused you great distress, right?"

"Yes, go on."

"In God's eyes, you are worth far more than that ring. He loves you, Annie, but His heart is sad because He created you to have fellowship with Him, but you are like that lost ring. You have great value in God's eyes."

"Me?" she said, her eyes pleading.

"Yes! He loves you! He's calling you into relationship with Him. He loves you so much that He spoke to my wife about you. Isn't that amazing?"

In total unbelief, she sat on her bed shaking her head. I could tell that the questions were racing through her mind: *Could this really be true? Does God really love me so much that He would send a policeman here to tell me?*

We talked some more until my shift ended. I gave her a copy of our personal testimony tract with our telephone number and encouraged her to contact me if she needed help. I came home and told Crissy the exciting news! She was encouraged that the Lord had used her to help reach this precious "lost ring."

* * *

About two weeks later, Annie called Crissy. She was still in jail, but shortly after leaving the hospital, she had prayed to

receive Christ as her Lord! She then told the whole story to her
husband, who also received Christ! Together, they started to
evangelize the entire prison population!

The Lord had given Crissy a word of knowledge that had
opened the hearts of Annie and her husband to really hear the
gospel. Supernatural ministry is a necessity in spreading and
confirming the gospel today.

Find Your Gifts

Paul urged us to earnestly desire spiritual gifts (see 1 Cor.
14:1). He understood not only the reality of spiritual gifts, but
their importance as well, including lists and discussion of gifts
in no fewer than three of his Epistles and mentioning them in
several others. The longest and most detailed discussion of
spiritual gifts in the writings of Paul is found in his first letter
to the Corinthians, where he devotes three entire chapters to
the subject. Early in his discourse, Paul describes the gifts:

> *Now to each one the manifestation of the Spirit is
> given for the common good. To one there is given
> through the Spirit the message of wisdom, to another
> the message of knowledge by means of the same
> Spirit, to another faith by the same Spirit, to another
> gifts of healing by that one Spirit, to another miracu-
> lous powers, to another prophecy, to another distin-
> guishing between spirits, to another speaking in
> different kinds of tongues, and to still another the
> interpretation of tongues* (1 Corinthians 12:7-10).

For ease of understanding, the gifts listed in these verses
may be classified into three different groupings:

- *The inspiration gifts*—speaking in tongues, inter
  pretation of tongues, and prophecy;

- *The revelation gifts*—the word of wisdom, the word of knowledge, and discerning of spirits; and
- *The power gifts*—faith, healing, and miracles.

Paul then discusses the importance that each person has as a member of the Body of Christ. There is one Spirit who gives the gifts as He wills, and each member of the Church has been gifted and has a vital ministry function in the Church. A little later he writes:

And in the church God has appointed first of all apostles, second prophets, third teachers, then workers of miracles, also those having gifts of healing, those able to help others, those with gifts of administration, and those speaking in different kinds of tongues (1 Corinthians 12:28).

In his letter to the Romans, Paul describes the gifts somewhat differently:

We have different gifts, according to the grace given us. If a man's gift is prophesying, let him use it in proportion to his faith. If it is serving, let him serve; if it is teaching, let him teach; if it is encouraging, let him encourage; if it is contributing to the needs of others, let him give generously; if it is leadership, let him govern diligently; if it is showing mercy, let him do it cheerfully (Romans 12:6-8).

A third listing of gifts is found in Ephesians. These are the *doma* gifts, the fivefold ministry gifts given for the building up and equipping of the Church:

It was He who gave some to be apostles, some to be prophets, some to be evangelists, and some to be pastors

*and teachers, to prepare God's people for works of
service, so that the body of Christ may be built up until
we all reach unity in the faith and in the knowledge of
the Son of God and become mature, attaining to the
whole measure of the fullness of Christ* (Ephesians
4:11-13).

Clearly, then, there is a wide range and diversity of gifts,
all given by the Holy Spirit as He wills. The basic purposes
of the gifts are to edify and build up the Church, equipping
us for ministry, and as confirming signs and wonders to
unbelievers.

Discovering our gifts is not as difficult as it may appear
at first. Usually we find ourselves drawn toward certain
gifts. Do you have a desire to move in the gift of healing?
Perhaps the Lord has put that desire in your heart. If that's
the case, pursue that gift. Don't sit back idly waiting for
God to simply drop it into your lap. Seek the *gift* and the
Giver. Be bold and ask God to allow you to function in that
gift. My wife didn't just *happen* to see a vision. She developed that gift over time as she grew in her relationship with
God. She had prophesied many times before in small group
settings, or at water baptisms, and learned how she could
reliably "see" and "hear" from God. It took time, experience, and lots of practice. Jack Deere writes in his book,
Surprised By the Power of the Spirit:

"Some people have a difficult time understanding how
you can develop a gift that is supernaturally empowered. This difficulty stems from viewing the miraculous
gifts as magical or mechanical. A teacher can grow in
the gift of teaching, and an evangelist can grow in the
gift of evangelism. Why is it difficult to believe that
someone can grow in the gift of healing or prophecy?
The truth is that we can grow in every spiritual exercise
and every gift."[1]

That is encouraging news. We can actually grow in and develop spiritual gifts. When I desired to grow in the gift of evangelism, I began to read every book on the subject that I could get my hands on. Then I wanted to be around people that operated in the gift. Whenever I got the chance, I would ask these people to pray for me. I was also sharing the gospel on a regular basis. I was practicing. The same was true with the gift of healing. Jesus promises us that if we seek, *and keep on seeking*, we will find. If we knock, *and keep on knocking*, the door will be opened to us! (See Matthew 7:7.)

Join a Short-Term Missions Team

One of the best ways to find and develop your gifts is to serve in your church or to participate on a short-term missions team in your own hometown, in other places in America, or overseas. I have been continually amazed during such trips to watch "average" Christians face greater challenges than ever before and to see them radically grow in their knowledge and exercise of their spiritual gifts.

I led a group of about 20 people from several different churches for two weeks of intensive ministry in post-Communist Romania. We arrived around dinner time on a Saturday in the Transylvanian region of Romania (yes, such a place truly exists). After eating dinner, we rounded up the group for a spontaneous time of street ministry in a square near our hotel. We sang a couple of songs to guitar accompaniment and found ourselves suddenly surrounded by a group of about 200 people. Even people from an Orthodox church across the street abandoned their meeting to come check us out!

I had warned a few team members to be ready to publicly share their testimonies through an interpreter. It was great to see these normal folks rising to the occasion and preaching on the streets in another nation. One brother, Kurt, transformed into a fiery preacher as he shared his testimony.

There was a tiger in him that wanted to get out. The Lord really used him on this trip.

After a few testimonies, Dr. Alan Throner, an M.D., gave a short message on healing, followed by an invitation to anyone there who wanted to receive prayer for healing. We were literally mobbed as about half of the crowd came streaming forward. We then formed prayer teams (everyone had to be involved) and prayed for these precious people. I will never forget personally praying for one elderly man. Because we had only one interpreter, we couldn't communicate with everyone we prayed with. There were simply too many! So I just laid my hands on this man and prayed. From the tears streaming down his face, it was obvious that God was touching him deeply. Many people testified of miraculous healings that night. We told the people we would be ministering at a local church the next morning, and we invited them to come.

When we arrived the next morning in front of the church, the elderly man whom I had prayed for the night before was waiting for us at the door. He ran up to me with a big smile on his face and shook my hand over and over. Through an interpreter he explained that he had suffered with extreme pain in his right arm and shoulder for many years. As I had prayed with him that evening, he realized that the pain was totally gone for the first time in years! That's why he had been crying! The memory of that day is forever etched upon my mind. He sat proudly in the first row of that church, singing with all his heart! I'm so happy we had that spontaneous street outreach the night before.

Experiences like these change our lives! Everyone on the team used his or her gifts and made a significant contribution to the team. Whether it was serving, helping, evangelism, prophecy, admonition, intercession, healing, drama, or even videotaping, everyone was important and had a role to play.

Do you sometimes feel like life is passing you by? Do you feel stuck in the mundane? Are you eager to use your gifts and step out into the supernatural realm? Join a short-term missions team! There are many organizations that have missions opportunities that can meet your budget and scheduling needs. Forward Edge, Y.W.A.M., and many others are looking for folks like you who have a desire to serve and do something radical for God!

You have gifts from the Lord and a significant role to play in God's Kingdom! Begin to explore and develop those gifts. Find a place of need in your church and *serve*. You will quickly see your gifts come forth. Do you feel drawn to certain gifts? Ask God to stir them up within you. Talk it over with your pastor or home group leader. Get into a discipleship group for that gift. Read books in those areas and pray daily that the Lord will give you opportunities to use that gift. As I was writing this chapter, I was asking God to further develop the healing gift within me. One night before I went to sleep I asked the Lord for more opportunities to pray for the sick and further develop the healing gift. Very early the next morning, the telephone woke us up. A sick church member "just happened" to call to ask me to come pray for him. That had rarely happened before! Start praying and God will give you plenty of opportunities. Ask God and He will *empower, encourage*, and *equip* you to operate in spiritual gifts! It's time to get out of the boat!

Endnote

1. Jack Deere, *Surprised By the Power of the Spirit* (Grand Rapids: Zondervan Publishing House, 1993), 165.

Chapter Twelve

To the Ends of the Earth

"Personal renewal leads to corporate revival. Only the corporate man can fulfill the vision for the church that is in the heart of God."

—Graham Cooke

"Holy Rollah," my Austrian friend Guenther said to me in his funny German accent. We laughed together as we watched a church member whom we had just prayed for literally roll in a large circle on the floor while laughing hysterically. Something had broken out in our church in Basel after we had begun praying for people. What was going on?

Toronto, Ontario: "The Toronto Blessing"

Since January of 1994, hundreds of thousands of people have streamed to Toronto to be filled and touched by the Spirit of God. Manifestations such as holy laughter, falling down, and drunkenness in the Spirit are the norm. Most of those who visit the Toronto Airport Christian Fellowship, which is pastored by John and Carol Arnott, leave with a greater sense of the presence of God, the love of God, and the mercy of God. They have a greater desire to spend time in His presence, to read the Bible, and to share with others about Jesus. Many broken and/or burned-out people come away refreshed, renewed, and filled with new hope for their lives and/or ministries.

My parents, Mati and Carol Tammaru, frequently visit the Toronto church and participate in many of the events held there. The ten-hour drive from Gaithersburg, Maryland, is no burden to them because they are always filled up and refreshed during their visits. They both come from very conservative and proper church backgrounds, so you can imagine how stunned they both were when they were overwhelmed by the power and love of the Holy Spirit in very literal physical manifestations.

My mother, who is a very proper and dignified lady, always nicely dressed and always maintaining control, has often been "drunk in the Holy Spirit" after meetings in Toronto. One evening she was wheeled out in a wheelchair and literally carried into the hotel! Likewise, my father, who had undergone heart bypass surgery about six years earlier, received "open-heart surgery" from the Holy Spirit as he literally lay on the carpet laughing uncontrollably for about an hour! This is quite unusual for a man who was born in Europe and is the typical stoic European. He maintains that the Lord was healing past wounds during that time. What is amazing, though, is the change in the depth of my parents' walk with God, their devotion, their love, and their desire to fulfill God's call in their lives! That is good fruit! If that is what's being served up in Toronto, then I want another drink!

Shortly after my parents had visited Toronto for the first time, my wife and kids visited them in Gaithersburg over the Thanksgiving holiday. I had to remain in Europe because of various responsibilities, but was scheduled to join them before Christmas. During this time, my parents encouraged Crissy to watch a videotape of Rodney Howard-Browne, the South African evangelist. As Crissy watched with my parents and saw different pastors become speechless and "drunk in the Spirit" she thought to herself, *Boy, these people are a little over the edge. I can't relate to this.* A little bored, she got up about halfway through the tape to call my sister Krista. Krista's husband Ray answered the phone. As Crissy wanted to ask for Krista, she mistakenly said, "Hello, Ray, this is

Krista." At that point, the Holy Spirit came upon Crissy, and she began laughing uncontrollably. She said that it just bubbled up out of her insides like a fountain. She was so filled with the joy of the Lord, she couldn't stop laughing. After a while, she just laid down on the floor and soaked in the presence of the Lord. Our daughter Stephanie came over to her, and the two of them prayed for a while. It was a wonderful experience of the loving presence of God the Father. What we didn't know was that a couple weeks later Crissy would have emergency surgery to remove an ovarian cyst. She says that the joy of the Lord she received during this time of laughter was a great comfort to her through the unexpected time of surgery and recovery. In these days God is revealing Himself as "Abba Father."

Pasadena, California

Dr. Ché Ahn also visited Toronto Airport Christian Fellowship. Badly needing refreshing and new direction himself, he was powerfully met by God. Returning to Pasadena, Ché met with some other pastors in the city and together they decided to invite John Arnott to come and minister in Pasadena. Renewal broke out at Mott Auditorium (U.S. Center for World Missions) with sightings of angels, miraculous healings, and other supernatural phenomena. Thousands have attended renewal meetings and conferences since 1995. The move of God was so significant that five churches merged to form Harvest Rock Church, which Ché leads as senior pastor. Since then, Harvest International Ministries (H.I.M.) has been formed to see the gospel preached to all nations. Ché believes that renewal is not an end in itself, but a means to reach our goal of preaching the gospel to every nation, tribe, tongue, and people. H.I.M. is an association of churches networking to accomplish this goal together. My church, Oikos International Church in Basel, is a part of this international network. All over the world today, churches, organizations, and individuals are linking up to work together to bring in the end-time harvest.

Pensacola, Florida: "The Brownsville Revival"

As of this writing, since June, 1995, over 140,000 people have reportedly converted to Christ in the Brownsville Assembly of God Church in Pensacola. In this town of only 120,000, unusual manifestations of the Spirit are accompanying the move of God. My wife and I visited Brownsville Assembly in April 1997. What struck us was the impact the revival was making in the community. As we drove in, we began seeing billboards from businesses welcoming people attending the "Brownsville Revival"! As we were shopping in a local bookstore, my wife asked the clerk what Brownsville used for their children's ministry curriculum. A man nearby overheard her question and came over to us. Looking like the proverbial "just dragged in by the cat" type, with a long, unkempt beard and hair and tattoos all over, he startled us when he said, "I know Brownsville!" He grinned broadly, displaying a mouthful of teeth badly needing repair. "I just got saved there last Friday night! I was trying to kill myself that day by throwing myself in front of cars, but they kept slowing down! Then I saw the long line outside of Brownsville Assembly, and I decided to check it out. That night I gave my life to Christ!"

We knew then that this revival was for real! Of course, we were still amazed as we watched the hundreds run forward for salvation or recommitment that evening during the service.

These phenomena, and many more like them, are happening around the world today. God is doing something wonderful. He is refreshing and renewing His Church, and preparing her for a coming revival that will be of such scope and magnitude that we can't even imagine it! What I find especially exciting is that this is happening in a *Western* culture. This is not China, or South America, or Korea—it's *North America*!

Understanding the Times

First Chronicles chapter 12 tells of the brave men who came to join David's army. These men possessed a very important characteristic of a people who are ready to engage the enemy:

Men of Issachar, who understood the times and knew what Israel should do... (1 Chronicles 12:32).

If we are to be effective in this hour as the people of God, His army, then it is imperative that we discern, know, and understand the times in which we live. Jesus actually rebuked the Israelites in Luke 12:54-57 for their lack of understanding:

He said to the crowd: "When you see a cloud rising in the west, immediately you say, 'It's going to rain,' and it does. And when the south wind blows, you say, 'It's going to be hot,' and it is. Hypocrites! You know how to interpret the appearance of the earth and the sky. How is it that you don't know how to interpret this present time? Why don't you judge for yourselves what is right? (Luke 12:54-57)

In other words, He was saying, "Look, you guys, you know how to interpret natural phenomena like the weather, stock markets, and such, but when the Messiah, the Anointed One, comes into your midst with healings, signs and wonders, and miracles, you are so thick-headed that you don't even realize who I am! You are missing a visitation of God Himself!"

Unfortunately, the same thing is happening today! God is in our midst, visiting His Church, and we are too dull to discern and understand it! Help us, Lord! The Anointed One has come to His Church, to bring renewal, refreshing, and fresh fire, so that we may be enabled to effectively reach a lost and dying world. But, like the pharisees of old who were so distracted with having "the correct doctrine" or the "correct protocol" or the fear of losing their place of prestige and power in the religious world, churches, movements, denominations, and individuals today are missing the present visitation of God. For example, the following are some common complaints and objections:

- "That laughing, shaking, and falling down stuff doesn't fit into our theology. God wouldn't do that. The Holy Spirit is a gentleman." (*Is He? Ask Paul what he thought about his encounter with God on the road to Damascus!*)
- "They aren't teaching correct doctrine there." (*Are people coming to know Jesus as Lord and Savior? Do they have a greater love for God and their neighbor?*)
- "Who are they to bring this to our city (or nation)? We have been here longer. They are just newcomers." (*If we waited for you to do something, we would still be waiting!*)
- "If this continues, all the people will start going to them. This is just a fad, but a dangerous one." (*Sound familiar? The Pharisees said the same: "If Jesus continues, the Romans will take away our place and our nation."*)

If we would spend as much time preaching the gospel as we do bickering among ourselves, the world would already be evangelized! I believe that God is presently visiting His Church in order to prepare her for the times that lie ahead: days of harvest as well as days of trials. This is just the beginning.

Revival or Judgment?

In 1991, Dr. David Yonggi Cho, pastor of Yoido Full Gospel Church (the largest church in the world), was praying for America in Seattle. He asked the Lord, "Will You judge

America?" The Lord answered, "I have not reserved America for judgment, but for revival." He then revealed to Cho that revival would begin in Pensacola, Florida, spread to Mobile and New Orleans, then sweep up the east coast, through the midwest, down to the southwest, up to the northwest until all America was touched by revival![1] On June 17, 1995, this revival broke out in Brownsville Assembly in Pensacola, Florida. What is going to happen in the days ahead?

There is a spiritual expectancy in the air. We are on the threshold of something so big and so fantastic that we cannot even imagine how it will affect the future of Christianity and the Church. We are about to witness the greatest outpouring of God's Spirit that the world has ever seen. Are we ready to receive it? The real adventure of revival is close at hand!

Recently one evening in April 1998, my wife and I were driving down the mountain where we live near Basel, Switzerland, after a cloudy and rainy day. As we rounded a curve in the road, I suddenly saw something in the heavens. Right in front of us a hole in the clouds had opened up in the perfect form of the United States of America. I said to Crissy, "Look, Crissy, it's a perfect map of America!" What was interesting, though, was that the sun was setting, and the hole in the clouds was a brilliant glowing orange/gold color, like fire. America was engulfed in flames! In the middle of America was a dark cloud, but from the southern half of Texas eastward to Florida, then north to Maine, then to the Great Lakes, and from Texas westward to California, then north to Washington State—all was aflame in this glorious orange.

When Bob Jones, a prophet in Charlotte, North Carolina, published his "Shepherd's Rod Prophecy for 1998," he declared that orange was the color for this year! He writes, "This orange was also the color of the setting sun. As it is written, 'It shall be light in the evening time' (Zech. 14:7). Much of what has been hidden will be uncovered this year, by those who draw close to Christ."[2]

The Purpose of Renewal and Revival

On the day of Jesus' ascension, He left the disciples with a promise:

...Do not leave Jerusalem, but wait for the gift My Father promised...in a few days you will be baptized with the Holy Spirit. ...you will receive power when the Holy Spirit comes on you; and you will be My witnesses...to the ends of the earth (Acts 1:4-5,8).

The main purpose of the baptism of the Holy Spirit was not speaking in tongues, prophesying, or acting like drunken men—all of which occurred ten days after Jesus made this promise. The main purpose was to empower the disciples to be witnesses throughout the world. That purpose has not changed. The renewal now underway must be used to empower God's people to become witnesses to a lost world. As people are being touched, healed, and "loved on" by their heavenly Father, they will respond by returning to their families, their jobs, their neighborhoods, and yes, to the world with the gospel of peace. If we miss this, we are missing the main point of renewal *and* the baptism in the Holy Spirit.

We Have a Job to Do

Every time I remember my meeting with Leroy, I am reminded anew of the urgency of the hour. Leroy's *eternal* life was in the balance. We almost missed it. By God's grace, Paul and I were able to share with him just before he died. In the same way, every day that we waste in idleness is gone forever. Our friends and families are dying. Our society is deteriorating around us at an astonishing rate. Terrorism is now in our own backyards. The moral fabric of our nations is disintegrating. We need a revival. It is our only hope. There are multitudes of "Leroys" depending on us—depending on you—to be faithful in prayer and in the sharing of our faith. There are three elements that are necessary for revival:

1. Repentance and prayer (2 Chron. 7:14).

2. A sovereign move of God's grace.

3. God's people mobilized and ready for war—taking back their lost territory. (We see this pattern throughout Judges, First and Second Kings, and First and Second Chronicles.)

The sequence is like this: We prepare through repentance and prayer; God responds with His mercy and grace; and then God's people defeat their enemies and go on a major offensive. Of the three elements, we are responsible for the first and third. God's sovereignty is up to Him. We respond to His grace and sovereignty and move out in His power. It seems clear that we are on the brink of a worldwide spiritual revival. We must now respond in prayer and in action to begin taking back the land that our enemy has stolen!

Repentance Through Prayer and Fasting

Another sign of our times is the increase of prayer and fasting in the Church. A few years ago, Dr. Bill Bright, the founder of Campus Crusade for Christ, felt the Lord call him to a 40-day fast. In the middle of the fast, the Lord spoke to him clearly that revival was coming, but that Christians worldwide needed to seriously heed God's call:

If My people, who are called by My name, will humble themselves and pray and seek My face and turn from their wicked ways, then will I hear from heaven and will forgive their sin and will heal their land (2 Chronicles 7:14).

He felt that the only way to fulfill the requirements of this verse was through prayer and fasting. At the same time, he also felt a call to challenge 2,000,000 believers to fast and pray for 40 days before the year 2000. Since that time, hundreds of thousands of Christians, and thousands of churches, have taken 40-day fasts, seeking God's face for revival. Let's face it: Drastic times require drastic measures. If the King of the universe had to fast 40 days before embarking on His ministry, how much more do we, His servants, need regular times of fasting and prayer to fulfill our service?

The last time there was a major call to prayer and fasting of a similar magnitude was in the 1940's. It is interesting to note that in that time the great "Voice of Healing" revivals were taking place with evangelists like William Branham, Gordon Lindsey, Oral Roberts, Jack Coe, F.F. Bosworth, and others. Then, in 1948, the nation of Israel was reborn. Coincidence? I don't think so. What God is doing in the natural with Israel, He is doing in the spiritual with the Church.

So now, 50 years after the founding of Israel (Jubilee year), millions of believers worldwide are participating in 40-day fasts! What will be loosed in the world? I believe it will be a great spiritual awakening, with signs and wonders of God as a major hallmark.

In the spring of 1997, our church participated in a 40-day fast. It was a wonderful time of seeking God's face and drawing near to Him. I know that many of the answers to our prayers are being released because of that time. It was a blessing spiritually and physically to us all. (My cholesterol even dropped from 250 to 137!)

I want also to say that I believe that *fasting is for every believer* (except in the cases of those with special medical problems). (Before embarking on any extended fast, one should first consult his pastor and doctor.) Dr. Bright's books, *The Coming Revival* and *The Transforming Power of Fasting and Prayer*,[3] have many practical tips regarding fasting and juice fasting. I highly recommend them. I had the privilege of meeting with Dr. Bright in January 1998, as he was here in Basel, Switzerland. Dr. Bright has now completed five 40-day fasts over the past four years. I asked him after the meeting if he was going to continue fasting 40 days every year, and if so, for how long. His answer is remarkable for someone who is 76 years old and has been in ministry for over 40 years:

> "I plan to fast 40 days every year, so long as I am phys-ically able to do it. And I would encourage you, young man, to consider the same, and to make fasting a part of your lifestyle."

Wow! What words of challenge from a real spiritual father in the faith. If we are serious about repentance and seeking the face of God for revival and healing in our lands, then we need to become serious about fasting and making fasting a lifestyle.

The Emerging Church: Unity

There is a fresh wind blowing in the Church today with regard to unity. For far too long, the Church has been *sub-merged*, but she is now *emerging* as His glorious Bride. Do you see the common word here? *Merge!*

Often the world picks up the voice of God long before the Church. It is sad, but in many instances the children of dark-ness are more discerning than the children of light. Take big-otry and racial reconciliation, for example. The world was preaching reconciliation long before the Church caught wind of it. Hollywood is often more prophetic than the Church. Current films with themes of nuclear terrorism (such as *Broken Arrow*, *The Peacemaker*) and natural catastrophes (such as *Outbreak*, *Dante's Peak*, *Volcano*, *Deep Impact*, and *Armegeddon*) speak of the judgments of God.

One thing the world has learned is the value of working together toward a common goal. Putting aside differences, many firms have teamed up or merged to fulfill their goal of making a buck.

In Basel this past year, two of the largest pharmaceutical companies, Ciba Geigy and Sandoz, merged to make Novartis. A few months later, two of the largest banks in Switzerland, Union Bank of Switzerland and Swiss Bank Corporation, merged into United Bank of Switzerland. Now, we have recently heard of the largest industrial merger in history, Daimler-Benz of Germany (maker of Mercedes Benz) and Chrysler Corporation of America. I know that banks are merging in the U.S. as well.

The people of God are beginning to hear as well. My friend Michael Horn always says, "I know that unity will one day come, because Jesus Himself prayed for unity among believers in John 17." Amen. Unity will come because it is the will of God and the prayer of Jesus.

Churches all over the world are beginning to lay down their differences and their pride and are starting to work together. Many are even beginning to merge. As I shared earlier, Ché Ahn's church merged with four other churches. They realized that they could better fulfill their call to reach the Los Angeles area together than apart. That meant sacrifices and adjustments for all of them. Rick Wright, who had been a senior pastor for over 15 years, laid down his leadership to come alongside Ché and serve with him. What's interesting, though, is that Rick had always felt a call to go to the nations, but his responsibilities as a senior pastor made it difficult to do. Since merging in ministry with Ché, he is now finally free to fulfill those dreams and has literally been traveling all over the world. He comes often to us here in Basel—another result of their merger.

This is not limited to America, however. Bob Jones' "Shepherd's Rod Prophecy for 1998" also mentions the coming together of Christians for a greater good. He writes, "I saw the Lord extinguish many little lights in order to bring forth one great concentrated light that will shine much more brightly."[4] After I read this, the Lord began to speak to me of merging together with like-minded churches in the city of

Basel. On June 7, 1998, my church, Oikos Fellowship, merged with International Christian Fellowship. Our "wedding" was wonderful as we exchanged "vows." I will serve the new church as senior pastor, and work together with Larwin Nickelson and his team to reach this city for Jesus. What we couldn't do alone due to limited resources, workers, and finances, we can now do together. I believe that this is a prophetic sign to the nations, where church splits and factions have been the norm, that God is bringing His Church together! The nation of Switzerland was founded over 900 years ago, when three small cantons formed an alliance. For the past nine centuries, Switzerland has enjoyed relative peace and remained a stable and blessed nation. I believe unity has played a key role in that.

It is time to work together again and restore the ancient walls that have been destroyed.

The Church's Responsibility

And this gospel of the kingdom will be preached in the whole world as a testimony to all nations, and then the end will come (Matthew 24:14).

Our responsibility has not changed. We have been given a commission to go as we have never gone before. We must take this command seriously, both as individuals and as churches. Paul Cain, a well-known prophet in the Body of Christ, recently had a dream concerning the need for the Church to arise in these last hours. The Lord said to him, "The only thing that will deliver the multitudes that are perishing is to engage the Church in immediate intercession and travail. *Don't waste any more time*—time is of the essence." He was told that we have a brief window of opportunity now to mobilize the Church to intercede for the next visitation of God. We need intercessors to pray for grace, for power, and for our protection, as well as that of our families, as we go on the offensive to call the Church back to New Testament standards of *inter-cession, holiness, sacrificial living (offering)*, and *prophetic ministry (IHOP)*. Believers, especially those in leadership, will be offering their lives, their time, their energy, and especially their finances for the Kingdom. Millions of dollars will flow in for the purposes of God. People will be giving sacrificially and will simplify their lifestyles so that they can do so.

> *Then the word of the Lord came through the prophet Haggai: "Is it a time for you yourselves to be living in your paneled houses, while this house remains a ruin?" Now this is what the Lord Almighty says, "Give careful thought to your ways. You have planted much, but have harvested little. You eat, but never have enough. You drink, but never have your fill. You put on clothes, but are not warm. You earn wages, only to put them in a purse with holes in it." This is what the Lord Almighty says: "…Go up into the mountains and bring down timber and build the house, so that I may take pleasure in it and be honored," says the Lord* (Haggai 1:3-8).

This is a word for the Church. We have a job to do, and we need to get to it. It's time to stop building our personal kingdoms, and time to give sacrificially to the work of God. We must preach the gospel to the world. If we would spend only a fraction of our finances on what we now spend for buildings, programs, and other perks, we would have plenty to preach the gospel to the nations. As individuals, if we would simplify our lifestyles and pray, God would show us how we could better give to world missions. The time is short! One day as we stand before the King of kings, we won't be remembering our new church buildings or material possessions. We'll be wondering if we could have sacrificed more so that His house would be fuller on that glorious day!

Where Do We Go From Here?

My prayer for you is that you are freshly motivated to give all that you have for God's glory and His purposes in the earth today. Don't settle for an average life in God! God has given you talents, whether it be ten, five, or one, and He expects you to use what you have 100 percent for His glory. Are you living radically for God? Or have you lost your first love? You can get that radical edge back. Respond to the Holy Spirit's prompting in those areas He reveals to you. Make changes in the areas where you know that you have compromised in your life. Begin praying as you have never prayed before. Go on an extended fast to seek His face. Get involved in a church that will *provoke* you to grow and *allow* you to use your gifts to the greatest potential. Pray about how you should be involved with world missions. Should you go on a short-term team? Should you support someone else who goes? If you are a leader, is your church reaching the world with the gospel—in your locale and to the ends of the earth? Is it a *priority* in your heart and also in your budget? Someone once said, "You will see a church's priorities when you see its budget."

Make a decision now to change. Overcome *selfishness* and *fear* in your life. *Prepare* yourself for the outpouring of God. Live every day *led* by the Holy Spirit. Learn to discern and listen for His voice. Find out His *sovereign purpose* for your life, and *fling* yourself into it. *Pray* and travail in prayer for your loved ones. Reach your *oikos* for Jesus. Get out of the boat today and begin *believing* God will use you in the *supernatural* realm. *Develop* your God-given gifts and go for it. Give it all that you've got! Yes, you may be "ordinary," but with God, you will do "extraordinary" things!

"He is no fool who gives what he cannot keep, to gain what he cannot lose."

—Jim Elliott

Endnotes

1. "The Brownsville Breakthrough," *Second Wind*, Summer 1996.

2. Bob Jones, "Shepherd's Rod Prophecy for 1998," *MorningStar Bulletin*, January 1998.

3. *The Coming Revival: America's Call to Fast, Pray, and "Seek God's Face"* (Orlando: NewLife Publications, 1995) and *The Transforming Power of Fasting and Prayer: Personal Accounts of Spiritual Renewal* (Orlando: NewLife Publications, 1997).

4. Bob Jones, "Shepherd's Rod Prophecy for 1998."

Appendix A

Priorities, Vision, and Goals— _____ (date)

My Priorities

1. My personal relationship with Jesus.
2. My relationship with my spouse and children.
3. My emotional and physical health.
4. My career.
5. My ministry in the church and community.

My Personal Areas of Development

1. Spiritual
2. Emotional/Relational
3. Physical
4. Intellectual
5. Financial

My Short-Term Personal Goals— _____
(next 3 months)

1. Spiritual—*Vision: To maintain and develop further intimacy with God through daily communion with Him.*

Devotional Bible Reading Goal:
Prayer Goal:
Evangelism:
Memorization Goal:
Fasting Goal:
Ministry in Church:

2. Emotional/Family—*Vision: To maintain snd sustain my emotional health and that of my family through the nurturing of my important relationships, and ensuring I have sufficient fun activities in life.*

Dates with my spouse _____ per week for romance, communication, and fun.
Daily leisure reading:
Play _____ (sport) _____ per week.
Family vacation:
Two days away alone with my spouse: _____ times per year.
Play _____ with my children _____ per month.
Ensure that _____ is our Sabbath day of rest.
Make planning time with my spouse _____ times per month.
Take each one of my children out alone _____ times per month.

3. Physical—*Vision: To achieve and maintain proper nutrition and health through a balanced diet and regular exercise.*

Reach _____ pounds by _____.
_____ minutes exercise _____ times per week.
Diet:
Other:
Other:
Other:

4. Intellectual—*Vision: To develop myself intellectually through the regular reading of books, magazines, listening to cassettes, and _____.*

Read at least _____ books per month.
Listen to at least _____ teaching cassettes per month.
Read/Study:
Learn foreign languages:
Career:
Other:

5. Financial—*Vision: To maintain financial integrity, acquire savings, grow in generosity and faith, and to obtain financial freedom (be debt-free).*

Make a budget.
Stay current and on time with all payments.

Other:

Begin saving _____ per month.

Have all debts paid in full by:

Be challenged to obey God and increase our giving, and believe Him for an increase!

Long-Term Goals

Spiritual:

Career:

Family:

Educational/Intellectual:

Financial:

Ministry:

Other:

Other:

Other:

Appendix B

Personal Testimonies

Erik's Story: From Karate to Christ

The large man lunged at me and yelled. I instinctively fell into a defensive stance and adrenaline began to flow through my veins. The attacker then punched with incredible speed toward my face. Reacting quickly, I spinned and jumped at the same time, executing a "spin kick," which used my left foot to knock the attacker's arm down and away. Continuing to turn another 180 degrees, I knocked his front leg out from under him with the back of my right leg. He fell with a sickening thud onto the ground. I then punched with full power toward his face. I stopped the punch an inch short of his nose and smiled down at him.

"Nice move, Erik," my friend said with a groan, looking up at me from his reclined position on the mat. "Now it's your turn." It was test day at Karate summer camp. We were performing "one-step" take-down routines as part of our test to receive the first grade brown belt—one step away from our coveted goal, the black belt. I hoped that with achieving black belt, I would receive the happiness and meaning in life that I was so desperately seeking.

Well, I did pass the test, and I received my brown belt with the black stripes on it. My friend did too. What I did not receive, however, was the security and peace that I was looking for. Deep inside of me was an emptiness that drove me toward something—anything—that would give me a reason for living.

I wanted something that would bring lasting joy and happiness. Insecurity wasn't new to me. Actually, it was something that I had grown up with. I was always proficient at sports. Karate was just an extension of that. I wanted to be accepted by people. Later in high school, I hung out with the "cool dudes" who smoked, drank, and partied. By the time I was in college, I had the reputation of being a "wild and crazy guy."

I had a good family, friends, money, and girlfriends, but I had no joy and peace in my life. Up until this point in my life, sports, partying, sex, and karate had brought me temporary fulfillment that was empty and without meaning. I was looking for something more. Instead of me finding "it"; *He* found me!

In August of 1981, a friend explained to me that I could have a personal relationship with God. I could know Him and His unconditional love for me if I would simply give my life completely over to Him. He loved me and accepted me for who I was, not for what I could do for Him. I prayed with my friend that evening on a jetty overlooking Long Island Sound, and the presence of God flooded over me. I had never known such peace and joy before, and it was finally mine!

Since that day, my life has not been the same. I'm not talking about religion or church, but about knowing a real and living person. His name is Jesus Christ, and He died on a cross 2,000 years ago for your sins and failures. He's longing for a relationship with you right now. He was gloriously resurrected three days after His death, and He lives today. I know this because I've met Him.

He Himself bore our sins in His body on the tree, so that we might die to sins and live for righteousness; by His wounds you have been healed (1 Peter 2:24).

He died for you too! If you're looking for meaning in your life, He's the answer. He's your Creator and that's what's missing. Come to Him today, and experience an abundant life for the first time! You won't regret it!

Chrissy's Story: From Fear to Freedom

Just like Erik, I came to a place in my life where I realized that only Jesus could meet the deepest needs of my heart and soul. My father was a pastor, so I had grown up attending church. I always had a desire to see and experience the supernatural, but that was lacking in my church. So I got involved with the occult and experienced power and prestige, but I also sensed evil there. It was in this time that Jesus revealed Himself to me. I was "born again," and my life drastically changed. My whole family was astounded by this change in me. Although Jesus filled me with a reason for living and a great joy and peace, there was an area of fear in my life that God wanted to touch—a fear of manic depression.

I was living in a constant fear that I would inherit this disease that had devastated the lives of my great-grandmother, grandmother, and mother. Would it reach me as well? Sometimes I had all the symptoms—feelings of grandeur followed by depression and even suicidal thoughts. Would I be hospitalized like my mother and her mother before her? No! God had other plans for me! He was about to do a spectacular miracle in my life. On the weekend of my graduation with a master's degree in social work, my parents and younger brother visited me in Washington, D.C. At church the next morning, my pastor announced that the Lord had spoken to him that Jesus was going to heal people who had inherited diseases! I went forward for prayer with trembling. The pastor, not knowing my problem, immediately said to me, "It's a chemical imbalance." That's the medical reason for manic depression! He called my mother and brother forward for prayer as well, and we wept together with joy, as the curse of generations was broken!

To this day, we have remained healthy physically and emotionally! God is a great God!

Whatever your problems may be, Jesus is a loving God, full of mercy and grace. You can trust Him and give your life to Him.

Please Contact Us!

If you would like more information regarding the ministry of Erik and Crissy Tammaru, and/or their missions organization, C.F.F.I. (Christian Family Fellowships International), or obtain a free monthly newsletter, please write to:

C.F.F.I.
P.O. Box 3153
Gaithersburg, MD 20885-3153
USA

Fax: (301) 840-2075

E-mail: CFFI_Tammaru@compuserve.com

Internet: http://ourworld.compuserve.com/
homepages/CFFI_Tammaru/

Destiny Image
New Releases

3:72

D *Destiny Image*
New Releases

CORPORATE ANOINTING
by Kelley Varner.
Just as a united front is more powerful in battle, so is the anointing when Christians come together in unity! In this classic book, senior pastor Kelley Varner of Praise Tabernacle in Richlands, North Carolina, presents a powerful teaching and revelation that will change your life! Learn how God longs to reveal the fullness of Christ in the fullness of His Body in power and glory.
ISBN 0-7684-2011-3 $9.99p

SECRETS OF THE MOST HOLY PLACE
by Don Nori.
Here is a prophetic parable you will read again and again. The winds of God are blowing, drawing you to His Life within the Veil of the Most Holy Place. There you begin to see as you experience a depth of relationship your heart has yearned for. This book is a living, dynamic experience with God!
ISBN 1-56043-076-1 $9.99p

HIS MANIFEST PRESENCE
by Don Nori.
This is a passionate look at God's desire for a people with whom He can have intimate fellowship. Not simply a book on worship, it faces our triumphs as well as our sorrows in relation to God's plan for a dwelling place that is splendid in holiness and love.
ISBN 0-914903-48-9 $8.99p
Also available in Spanish.
ISBN 1-56043-079-6 $8.99p

Available at your local Christian bookstore.

Internet: http://www.reapernet.com